STOP HIDING!

10 Proven Strategies for Facing Debt Collectors Head On!

Netiva Floyd, MBA, CCC®

(The Frugal CrediTnista)

Table of Contents

Are Collection Agencies Legal? 8

"Debt Collections Are Necessary"..16

FDCPA - Debts Not Covered..20

FDCPA – Summary of Rights 21

FDCPA – Violators..23

Types of Debt Collectors 23

Type of Debts Collected On...24

How Debt Collectors Find You...25

The Dunning Letter...28

The Initial Telephone Call 35

Cease & Desist Letter 45

Statute of Limitations on Debt (SOL) 47

Acknowledgment of the Debt 51

The Validation Process..54

Validation Defined 54

Validation Letter...55

I've Sent the Letter, Now What?..59

Reviewing the Validation Responses 60

The 'Other' Side of Validation 69

Your Plan B..73

Where to Send Complaints 78

Most Common Violations 80

Summary of Steps 84

Conclusion 89

Appendix – Collection Dispute Letters.....................................92

Appendix - FAIR DEBT COLLECTIONS PRACTICES ACT 110

§ 801. Short Title [15 USC 1601 note]..............................110

§ 802. Congressional findings and declarations of purpose [15 USC 1692]...110

§ 803. Definitions [15 USC 1692a]...............................111

§ 804. Acquisition of location information [15 USC 1692b]..113

§ 805. Communication in connection with debt collection   [15 USC 1692c]...114

§ 806. Harassment or abuse [15 USC 1692d]...............116

§ 807. False or misleading representations [15 USC 1692e] 117

§ 808. Unfair practices [15 USC 1692f].............................119

§ 809. Validation of debts   [15 USC 1692g]...................121

§ 810. Multiple debts [15 USC 1692h] 122

§ 811. Legal actions by debt collectors   [15 USC 1692i] 122

§ 812. Furnishing certain deceptive forms [15 USC 1692j] 123

§ 813. Civil liability [15 USC 1692k] 123

§ 814. Administrative enforcement   [15 USC 1692l]....125

§ 815. Reports to Congress by the Commission [15 USC 1692m]...127

§ 816. Relation to State laws [15 USC 1692n]...............128

§ 817. Exemption for State regulation   [15 USC 1692o] 128

§ 818. Effective date [15 USC 1692 note] 128

Appendix – Statute of Limitations (Section of State's Legislature Included)..130

Resources..136

About the Author

Hello! My name is Netiva "The Frugal CrediTnista" Heard; I'm a Certified Credit Counselor, Personal Finance Coach, Illinois Real Estate Broker with a Master's in Business Management and Finance. I'm the owner of MNH Credit Solutions, a financial services firm out of Illinois that specializes in teaching their clients to Destroy their Debts, Grow their Money and Soar their Credit Scores. MNH Credit Solutions is where *Credit Transformations* happen!

I've been a Realtor for over 13 years, and have encountered so many people that have had to put their dreams of homeownership on 'pause' due to the negative items reporting on their credit reports. When I opened MNH Credit Solutions in 2008, my goal was to provide my clients with the tools, knowledge and resources needed to resolve their credit woes and to reclaim their dream of home ownership with the best interest rates and terms on the market. Over the years, due to personal experiences, intense education, and evaluating the true needs of my community, that goal has expanded to empowering my clients with the tools they need to achieve ALL of their financial goals.

This is the first book in my "Credit Makes $ense" Collection and I'm super excited to offer it to you. It is based on the premise of my entire business model: To Educate, Equip, Empower and Transform ☺.

I honestly receive more questions on how to effectively deal with collections more than any other item reporting on our credit reports. These questions include:

1. How to handle collection telephone calls?
2. How should I respond to the letter(s) they sent me?
3. Are collections legal?
4. What is a validation letter and when should I send one?
5. What constitutes proper validation?
6. Did a collection agency violate my rights?
7. What *are* my rights when it comes to dealing with a collection agency?

I will address these concerns and more, with the hopes that by the time you complete this guide, you will no longer question what to do when faced with a phone call, letter, or account listed on your credit report from a collection agency; you'll know! Financial literacy is **POWER!**

So... are you ready????? Let's go!

Are Collection Agencies Legal?

Collections have been around for as long as businesses have been accepting payment for goods and services. Yep, that long. Most would state that debt collectors should be banned in all 50 states and the entire industry should be dismantled, and at one point in my life I agreed whole-heartedly. You see, I'm MNH Credit Solutions' first client. I have literally had almost every type of debt collector coming after me; from medical to federal to private to public; I've had them all! I absolutely despised them. I did not like the arrogant, condescending and out right ignorant tone they took as if I personally called them up, borrowed money from them, and *intentionally* didn't pay it back. Who does that? And more importantly, why are you calling me? I didn't borrow anything from YOU!

Because of their underhanded tactics to seduce unwitty, financially illiterate and gullible consumers, many begin to question the legality of the entire industry. I often get, "These type of actions cannot be legal!" So, let's address this first.

Are Collection Agencies Legal?

I hear a lot of chatter about the collection industry being fraudulent, how they have no right to collect on our debts or to report anything on our credit report without our permission, and that's just the start of it! I'll be honest. There are laws out there that both support and negate the legality of the collection industry.

When a debtor defaults on a financial agreement, both the creditor and the debtor (you), have rights and duties during the collection process. They are usually outlined in the original contract itself, as well as in the state and federal laws pertaining to the collection of a debt; these include the Fair Debt Collection Practices Act, the Unfair Practices Act, the Universal Commercial Code, the Collection Agency Regulatory Act, and a few others.

On most of the contracts we sign when applying for credit, there's verbiage of the creditor's right to assign, transfer and/or sell the debt and our *lack* of the right to assign, transfer and/or sell the debt. Here's an example below from a popular credit card company:

Assignment

This Agreement will be binding on, and benefit, any of your and our successors and assigns. You may not sell, assign or transfer your *Account* or this Agreement to someone else without our written permission.

We may sell, assign or transfer your *Account* and this Agreement without your permission and without prior notice to you. Any assignee or assignees will take our place under this Agreement. You must pay them and perform all of your obligations to them and not us. If you pay us after we notify you that we have transferred your *Account* or this Agreement, we can return the payment to you, forward the payment to the assignee, or handle it in another way that is reasonable.

Pretty cut and dry, huh? Not really ☺.

There are a lot of loopholes that exist in our laws, which can create consumer confusion and misinformation being provided by so called credit 'experts'. Let's look at the top 3 arguments both for and against the legality of the debt collection industry:

You didn't sign a contract with the collection agency; thus you do not owe them.

Argument: The Universal Commercial Code – §3-203 TRANSFER OF INSTRUMENT; RIGHTS ACQUIRED BY TRANSFER

(a) An instrument is transferred when it is delivered by a person other than its issuer for the purpose of **giving to the person receiving delivery the right to enforce** the instrument.
(b) Transfer of an instrument, whether or not the transfer is a negotiation, **vests in the transferee any right of the transferor to enforce the instrument**.

Frugal CrediTnista's Notes: Transferee = Collection Agency. Transferor = Original Creditor

The Law of Assignment allows a creditor to assign or transfer their rights to another party, referred to as an 'assignee'. If a contract is involved, as it is with debt collection activities, the assignment includes both the rights and the benefits that the borrower had with the original creditor. The intentions of your creditor must be clear in the assignment agreement, and in case you're wondering – NO – you do *not* need to be notified of this assignment beforehand. The idea is that your duties, rights, and obligations remain intact and that the only thing that changes is to whom you now have those duties, rights, and obligations with; to what extent should be outlined in the terms of the assignment agreement(s).

The contract, therefore, needs to exist between your original creditor and the collection agency, not you. It must contain all the elements of a valid contract and state specifically the intentions and motives of the assignor – your original creditor – and what rights they are assigning/transferring to the collection agency – a portion of them or all of them.

1. I don't have a signed contract with the credit card company, everything was completed over the phone or online.

   Argument: You signed electronically or gave your consent over the recorded phone call and you used the funds, and quite possibly paid some of your monthly payments. You may not have a traditional written contract, but please believe you have an enforceable and valid contract. In 2000, the Electronic Signature in Global and International Commerce Act was passed that legalized both electronic contracts and electronic signatures.

   Some states have adopted the Uniform Electronic Transactions Act that legalizes electronic signatures and contracts as well. Check your state laws to see if they have adopted this Act, and what contracts fall under it. If there are significant differences between your state and the federal law; federal ranks supreme.

   To add, many are aware of both verbal and written agreements, but most states recognize implied contracts as well. Namely, if your actions imply that a contract exists or that you are in agreement with the terms and conditions of a contract without a 'wet' signature, then an enforceable contract exists. You used the card, accepted and utilized the funds, you paid some monthly bills – you have a contract.

2. The debt has been charged or written off, so it's already been paid!

   Argument: Written/Charged off does not mean PAID OFF, it also doesn't mean the debt has been forgiven. It's an accounting term that means the creditor isn't including your account (accounts receivables) as a part of their assets anymore. It's required by law so as not to mislead investors of their true earnings/value. Unless you've gotten a 1099 with verbiage that the debt is forgiven, expect your creditor to still pursue you for the debt.

So, what is a good argument <u>against</u> the collection industry? This one:

<u>The insurance that most accounts have on them.</u>

Yes, your creditors, particularly credit card companies, usually have insurance on your debt, and if you default the insurance will pay them after the 90 day mark. So, your creditor receives a small tax credit (not the full amount of the debt, so that's nothing to get happy over); they get paid by their insurance company; AND they can sell your debt to a debt collector. Hmm, somebody's getting the short end of the stick --- YOU!

If the creditor has gotten paid by their insurance, the debt should be satisfied, right?

I think so. This is called accord and satisfaction. If anyone should be pursuing you for payment, it should be the insurance company and not a debt collector, in my opinion. The insurance company suffered a loss, and therefore has the right of 'subrogation'. Whereas the debt collector is a mere 'stranger' to the debt. What do these terms mean?

Subrogation is when one entity substitutes their position for another one. Basically, the insurance company should be taking the position of the original creditor, since they paid the debt, and thus should be granted all of the claims, benefits and rights that the original creditor had per the terms of the original contract. Most subrogation claims pertain to the insurance industry; but certain actions can be taken to cause them to fall under debt collections laws as well.

To further support the above argument, consider 73 American Jurisprudence, 2nd Edition Section 93 under subrogation:

> "Subrogation will not be allowed to a third person who without any obligation to do so pays an indebtedness, and this rule is fully applicable to payments of an indebtedness secured by a mortgage." (The third person is the collection agency).

> "The right of subrogation does not exist for a stranger to the transaction" (The debt collector is a 'stranger to the transaction').

This is by far the best argument I've seen for the illegality of debt collections. Does it matter? Will knowing this crush the collection industry and wipe away thousands of 'fraudulent' debts?

Debt Collectors - A Necessary Evil?

"Debt Collections Are Necessary"

I once heard a CEO state that collection agencies help them save their current customers' money. His rationale was that if they were to not pursue their delinquent customers for payment of their unpaid debts, they'd have to pass those losses on to their other customers. As a consumer who now pays their bills in a timely fashion; I'm not trying to hear that! He went on to state that by taking such measures (hiring debt collectors), it deters regular paying customers from becoming delinquent out of fear of the consequences.

Now, I don't know about all that. Most people don't intentionally decide to stop paying their bills, either some life changing event happened; i.e. divorce, death of a loved one/spouse, job loss, medical illness; or they let their spending habits completely get the best of them and by the time they realize they are in over their heads, it's too late.

As a business owner, I can agree that if I have accounts receivables that have not been collected on and I have no other recourse but to write it off as a loss and calculate that into my business projections moving forward, I'll have to make up those losses through my current customers in order to remain profitable. That's business.

As a business owner, I can also understand outsourcing the collection of my past due accounts receivables so that I can focus on further marketing and expansion efforts.

I can also relate to wanting to write off my accounts receivables and selling the debt to another entity so that I can at least recoup some of my losses, move on, and again focus the bulk of my efforts on business growth.

Looking at this from an economic standpoint; the Urban Institute released a study in July 2014 that found that 35% of Americans have debts and unpaid bills that have been transferred over to a collection agency. That's a LOT!

To add, collection agencies employ over 140,000 workers who collect on roughly **$50 BILLION PER YEAR** (2014 study by the Federal Reserve's Philadelphia bank branch). Why am I telling you this?

Because so many people focus on whether the collection industry is illegal that they fail to realize that our government will never do anything to permanently eradicate them from the marketplace. They're too lucrative for our economy.

Laws may exist to protect our consumer rights; but ultimately our government is more concerned about solvency and profits. Don't believe me? Who did they bail out during our most recent recession? It sure wasn't us! Their reasoning was that the sooner businesses were able to bounce back, the sooner they'd start hiring again, providing loans again to help small to medium sized businesses and to re-stimulate the economy to prevent us from going into another Great Depression. In some cases it worked, others it didn't; we won't get into that. We will get into the fact that $50 billion pumped into the US economy each year is too good of a thing to pass up. Legal or not; collections are here to stay. Instead of worrying about fighting the legalities of the collection industry; I'd focus more so on:

1. Learning how to properly manage the money coming into your household, building up an emergency fund to better protect yourself against difficulties that affect everyone at some point in their lives, and becoming as financially educated as possible about your consumer rights so that when 'life happens' you will not be taken advantage of when/if a debt collector does come crawling your way.

2. Learning your consumer rights under your state collection laws, federal collection laws (FDCPA) and the Fair Credit Reporting Act (FCRA) so that you can easily spot violations and utilize them for leverage to remove them from your credit reports and possibly receive monetary damages.

I will give you tips on how to spot those violations and how to utilize them to your advantage. I have also included a copy of the Fair Debt Collection Practices Act (FDCPA) in the Appendix Section for your review; in addition to specific past case laws that I utilize and have referenced throughout this guide.

Debt Collectors & The FDCPA

FDCPA - Debts Not Covered

The information provided in this guide was written to assist with the debt collectors that are specifically covered under the FDCPA. This includes personal debts, familial debt, and household debts, which include money owed on a personal credit card account, an auto loan, a medical bill, and your mortgage. This guide will not assist with debts being collected on by the original creditor, business debts, agricultural debts, tax debts, and child support debts.

NOTE: There are some states that do include original creditors in their Collection Laws. This guide is based on Federal Collection Practices, but I would be remiss if I did not mention the states that have provided consumers protection from original creditors under their Collection Laws; they are: Arkansas, California, Connecticut, Florida, Iowa, Kansas, Louisiana, Maine, Maryland, Massachusetts (the _best_), Michigan, New Hampshire, New York, North Carolina, Oregon, Pennsylvania, South Carolina, Texas, Vermont, West Virginia and Wisconsin. There are a few states, such as Massachusetts, that require validation documents from original creditors as well.

Please review your state's Collection Laws for more detailed information.

FDCPA – Summary of Rights

- Collection agencies cannot discuss your debt with anyone other than you (more on this later in the text)
- Collection agencies must inform you that they are attempting to collect a debt when they first communicate with you and that any information obtain will be used for that purpose.
    - They must tell you their name and the collection agency's name as well, on later phone calls.
- Collection agencies may not contact you before 8a and after 9p.
- Collection agencies may not contact you directly if you are being represented by an attorney.
- Collection agencies may not contact you at work if they know your employer disallows it (you can tell them you are not allowed to receive personal phone calls at work to halt phone calls as well).
- Collection agencies are not allowed to use violence, threaten to use violence, harm you or threaten to harm you.
- Collection agencies are not allowed to use obscene, profane or abusive language.
- Collection agencies are not allowed to list your debt for sale to the public.
- Collection agencies are not allowed to publish your name as a delinquent bill payer (except child support collection agencies).

- Collection agencies cannot call you repeatedly or place phone calls to you without identifying themselves as a bill collector.
- Collection agencies cannot claim to be law enforcement, an attorney, a part of any government agency – state or federal.
- Collection agencies cannot falsely represent the amount you owe or the amount they will be paid for collecting on your debt.
- Collection agencies cannot claim that you'll go to jail or that you have committed some kind of crime for failing to pay a debt.
- Collection agencies cannot report false information to the credit bureaus.
- Collection agencies cannot use a false business name – over the phone or in writing - so as to deceive you.
- Collection agencies cannot add any other fees or charges that contradict your agreement with the original creditor, or your state laws.
- Collection agencies cannot accept a postdated check that is dated more than 5 days in advance UNLESS they notify you between 3-10 days of when they will be cashing it.
- Collection agencies cannot deposit a postdated check prior to the date on the check.
- Collection agencies cannot threaten criminal activity if you refuse to give them a postdated check for a debt.
- Collection agencies cannot communicate with you via postcards or put any other verbiage or symbol on an envelope that might let others know that they are attempting to collect on a debt.

This is just a summary, for a full description of your rights under the FDCPA, please see the full text in the Appendix Section, or visit the Federal Trade Commission's website.

FDCPA – Violators

If any of your rights have been violated per the FDCPA, a collection agency is on the hook for:

- Statutory Damages - $100 to $1000
- Punitive Damages
- Your Attorney Fees
- Regulatory fines – up to $2500
- Actual damages – emotional stress, damage to credit rating, defamation of character (reputational & humiliation damages), out of pocket expenses incurred by the Plaintiff

Do you see why it's important to focus on violations? They are awesome for leverage. You can pursue FDCPA violators up to 2 years from the time you discovered the violation or 5 years from the time the cause of action (or lack of action) that led to the violation arose.

Types of Debt Collectors

There are two primary types of collectors you'll encounter – A 3rd party debt collector and a debt buyer.

A 3rd party debt collector is hired to collect on a debt on behalf of a business. They get paid roughly 15-50% of the amount they collect, which means they *only* get paid when/if they collect. Some of their contracts will detail compensation for other services performed, such as skip tracing (finding you), long-distance phone calls, documents generated, etc.

Debt buyers collect on debts they have purchased from your original creditor or from another collection agency. They are often referred to as junk debt buyers because they typically purchase debts that other entities consider 'uncollectible' or that are past state and federal statute of limitations. They purchase the debt for pennies on the dollar, and now they want to get a return *and* profit by harassing you for payment.

Type of Debts Collected On

Most debt collectors are hired to collect on unsecured debts; meaning the debt is not secured by any type of asset or collateral. For example, a secured debt is when you purchase a home, the lender pays for the home (the loan) and sets up a contractual agreement where you will pay them back over the next 30 years at a specific interest rate, with your house being the 'security' for the debt. Basically, if you stop paying they can take the house, sell it and recoup some of their current and/or future losses.
An unsecured debt isn't secured by anything; you stop paying and the only measures they have to get their money back is to close the account, damage your credit score or sue you, which we'll discuss in detail later on. Because collection activities are so limited to these three areas, debt collectors will go to extreme measures – even violating your consumer rights – to collect on the debt.

How Debt Collectors Find You

I've often had clients receive a letter in the mail or a phone call at their job and wonder: "How the heck did they get this number or mailing address?"

The first place a collector will look is the information you provided the original creditor on your credit/loan application. Next, they look at your credit report to see if your personal information has been updated - mailing address, employer, telephone numbers, etc.

If they are not successful in finding updated information there, they use other methods,which include:
- hiring a 3rd party company to search for you (skip tracers),
- searching voter registration records,
- searching your state's moter vehicle department's database,
- searching the U.S. Postal Service for forwarding address information,
- looking at your social media profiles (set them to private to protect yourself);
- performing internet searches,
- hiring data aggregators (companies that gather information on consumers for marketing purposes),
- phone books,
- pretexters (companies that obtain information fraudulently – surveys are the most common tactic used.)
- family, friends, neighbors
- YOU!

The less a collecton agency knows about your income and assets the better. You do, however, want them to have your updated mailing address; which I'll explain in more detail as we move along.

Debt Collectors & The Dunning Letter

The Dunning Letter

The initial contact from a debt collector will start with a telephone call or a letter; each will try to create a sense of urgency in order to collect on the most debts in the least amount of time. I'll explain the telephone call in the next section, for now, let's tackle the dunning letter.

A dunning letter is simply a written notification of your debt that can be sent via fax, email, mail or in some cases a text message asking you to contact them to make payment arrangements.

This letter must include the following:

- That they are contacting you to collect the debt
- That any information obtained by you can be used in order to collect on that debt
- The name, number and address of the collection agency
- The specific amount you owe
- The name of the original creditor
- The right to dispute the debt for validity within 30 days, AND that if you do not dispute it within 30 days it will be considered valid
- That if you do dispute the debt, they will obtain the documentation to verify the debt and forward it to you
- Inform you of your right to request the name of the original creditor if they purchased the debt from another entity (another collection agency for example) if requested in 30 days

A lot of information can be obtained from this dunning letter so, really look over it. If the amount they are asking for is more than the original debt was when you became delinquent, the dunning letter should state why. This is referred to as 'Miller' language. Here's an example:

> "As of the date of this letter, you owe $500. Due to interest, late charges, and other charges that may vary from day to day, the amount due on the day you pay may be greater. Therefore, if you pay the amount shown above, an adjustment may be necessary after we receive your check, in which event we will inform you before depositing the check for collection."

Whether your letter states this or not; you have a right to demand a full accounting – basically a line-by-line itemization of purchases and charges from the moment the account was opened until it was charged off and purchased - to ensure it meets the terms within your contract, and in some cases your state's requirements. You would do this during the dispute for the validation period mentioned in the letter.

Why do you need this? Because it is illegal for a collection agency to make *"...false representation of – (A) the character, **amount**, or legal status of any debt; or (B) any services rendered, or compensation, which may be lawfully received by any debt collector for the collection of a debt (FDCPA 809. (2)(A) – See Appendix - FDCPA."*) Basically, they can't just tell you how much you owe, they have to SHOW you how much you owe.

In the letter, the notification of your right to dispute should be large, conspicuous, easily readable and easily noticeable. It should not be overshadowed by any other verbiage in the letter.

You will want to carefully review the letter to see if Overshadowing has occurred. This is when a debt collector will inform you of your right to dispute the debt and in the next sentence state something totally different. As an example, I've copied a snippet from a lawsuit; Chauncey v. JDR Recovery Corp., 118 F.3d 516 (7th Cir. 1997); where overshadowing occurred:

> "Dear Carl P. Chauncey,
>
> Please be advised that we have been requested by [Bridgestone/ Firestone] to assist them in the collection of the amounts due set forth above. Unless we receive a check or money order for the balance, in full, within thirty (30) days from receipt of this letter, a decision to pursue other avenues to collect the amount due will be made. Unless you notify this office within thirty (30) days after receiving this notice that you dispute the validity of this debt, or any portion thereof, this office will assume this debt is valid. If you notify this office in writing within thirty (30) days from receiving this notice that you dispute the debt or any portion of it, this office will obtain verification of the debt or obtain a copy of the judgment and mail you a copy of such judgment or verification. If you request this office in writing within thirty (30) days after receiving this notice, this office will provide you with the name and

address of the original creditor if different from the current creditor."

Did you guys catch that? In the 1st paragraph they asked for payment within 30 days of receipt from the dunning letter, and in the next paragraph they stated that the consumer had 30 days to dispute the debt. Really? The Court of Appeals found that the first paragraph contradicted the 2nd paragraph: *"We believe that the contradictions in the letter... would leave an unsophisticated consumer confused as to what his rights are and therefore violate the FDCPA."*

If you see the terms *immediately, quickly, urgent* on your dunning letter, that's a possible violation (Johnson v. Revenue Mgmt. Corp (1999); Ozkaya v. Telecheck Services (1997)).

If these words are bolded, capitalized, written in large font, italicized, that's a possible violation as well (Miller v. Payco-General American Credits, Inc., 943 F.2d 482, 484 (4th Cir. 1991)).

If the collection agency threatens action (reporting to credit bureaus, legal action, etc.) that will occur before or during the same time as your 30 day right to dispute, that's a possible violation ((Bartlett v. Heibl, 128 F.3d 497 (7th Cir. 1997); Graziano v. Harrison, 950 F.2d 107 (3d Cir. 1991)).

If you receive one letter from the collection agency providing your right to dispute within 30 days, and they send subsequent letters demanding payment or threatening legal action during that same 30 day timeframe; that's a possible violation (Johnson v. Revenue Mgmt. Corp., 169 F.3d 1057 (7th Cir. 1999)).

If you receive your Gramm-Leach-Bliley Act privacy notice in the same letter or the same envelope as your dunning letter, that's a possible violation (Hernandez v. Midland Credit Management, Inc., (2007)).

Your right to dispute for validation cannot be overshadowed by any other verbiage on the letter so as to not create confusion. It is your most important right under the FDCPA. It exists so that consumers will not be liable for debts that have been paid already, or that may not be theirs. For that reason, your right to dispute should be <u>conspicuous</u>, <u>noticeable</u> and completely <u>understandable</u> without any other items within the letter deterring you from exercising that right.

Your main objective when reviewing the dunning letter is to look for violations of the FDCPA from the very beginning. I call this 'Stacking Violations'. Violations are a great way to remove collections, settle for a much lower price than they offer you, or to sue for compensation that in some cases exceeds the original cost of the debt being collected.

Therefore, look for verbiage stating that any form of collection activity – to call in right away to avoid further collection activity, demand for payment, account repercussions due to not paying, threats of legal action – will take place within that 30 day right to dispute period; again this can create confusion to the consumer and it also violates your 30 day right to dispute for verification.

Who's the consumer? YOU. So, if you see this; act 'unsophisticated', create a file, file the letter and begin stacking your violations. **NO COLLECTION ACTIVITY SHOULD TAKE PLACE DURING THE 30 DAY VERIFICATION 'SAFE ZONE'.** Take advantage of this period. So many people throw this letter away when this is the very piece of documentation needed to get rid of them; or at the very least allow you to gain the upper hand!

Debt Collectors – Initial Telephone Call

The Initial Telephone Call

Collectors who decide to call you as their first point of contact take a huge risk. Number one, most will not inform you of your 30 day right to dispute the debt and number two they obtain payment of the debt without providing you with any of the information on the account as detailed above. You have a right to this information by law – FDCPA - whether this information is in writing or over the phone. Unfortunately, collection agencies will take this risk because it has brought them success over and over again. The reason why they have had so much success using this strategy is because so many of us are unaware of our rights. Man, are we going to change that!

When you receive a call from a collection agency, your main objective should be to get off the phone. Their main objective is to get you to pay. See the conflict? Gather specific information and IMMEDIATELY GET OFF THE PHONE.

Here's what a collection agency must do prior to disclosing any information regarding your account with them:

(A) Make sure that they are talking to you and NOT anyone else (it's a violation to tell anyone else, other than your attorney, about your debt),

   a. Per the FDCPA, the collector cannot disclose any info about your debt to anyone except: your spouse, if a minor, your parent(s) or guardian, your attorney, the credit bureaus, the original creditor and their attorney, the debt collector's attorney.

i. During their conversation with a 3rd party, they can only state their name - company name cannot be provided unless asked directly, any information on the debt can never be provided - collector must state that they are calling to obtain information about your whereabouts only. They are not allowed to call more than once unless they believe that the information originally provided was incomplete or wrong, _and_ that the person contacted has the correct information (this is B.S., in my opinion).

(B) Tell you who they are and where they are calling from (company),

(C) Tell you that the purpose of their call is to collect a debt and any information obtained during this call will be used for that purpose – Umm wait. Did you catch that? *ANYTHING YOU SAY DURING THIS PHONE CALL WILL BE USED AGAINST YOU TO COLLECT ON THIS DEBT.* This is why I said to get off the phone!

(D) Give you the details of the debt – name of the original creditor, amount of the debt, any other charges added, etc.

As I mentioned, I have not heard of one debt collector informing you of your 30 day right to dispute over the phone. More than likely you will need to bring this up. Legally, after initially contacting you over the phone, they should send you a dunning letter within 5 days. They will never mention this, and I have heard of some debt collectors lying and saying they sent it already, or that they don't have to send anything or flat out refusing to send it.

After they collect your personal information and inform you about the debt, they will immediately begin asking questions pertaining to your income, assets, investments, expenses and more. Get off the phone before that happens. This information benefits them, NOT you. Remember, anything you say can be used against you in an attempt to collect on the debt. Keep your mouth S-H-U-T.

Debt collectors are not privy to your non-public asset information unless it's on the paperwork you signed with the original creditor. It is your job to ensure that it stays that way. Their goal is simply to know IF and WHY you can't pay the debt and to obtain viable ways (in their minds) that you can pay the bill.

This is when you'll hear comments like:

"If you can tell me your income, I can see if you qualify for a lower payment amount."

"Who's your employer; we need your work number for our records (don't you dare tell!)"

"Can you borrow from your 401k?"

"Can you sell something?"

"Are you able to take out a personal loan, I'd hate to have to escalate this to a more aggressive form of collection activity (code for suing you)."

Don't even let it get to this point. Gather the information YOU need, and get off the phone. The following is the data you should be obtaining from each phone call with a debt collector.

Although you can't help being caught off guard with a collection call, if you are getting voicemail messages from them, you know it's inevitable that they'll eventually catch you on the phone. Be smart about protecting yourself. Remember, you're stacking violations; you can do this more efficiently by having proof of their violations in writing or via a voice recording.

You can record your conversations either with an old school recorder or a phone app (search your app store, there are plenty). Check your state laws on the permissions required when recording phone calls (www.rcfp.org), but remember, if they are recording you, there is no reason you should not be able to record them as well. Be smooth about it. As soon as they call and state: This call is being recorded; blah blah.... I intercede with *"Oh, good idea, I'll record the conversation for my records as well, is that okay?"* They'll either hang up or agree. If they disagree, simply ask why and demand that you don't consent to being recorded either. Again, they'll hang up or agree. If they lie about some state law and you can't record them, that's B.S.; don't fall for it. Call them on it and state firmly you'll be recording the call.

Other than harassing you with phone calls and letters, remember that there are only 3 actions a collection agency can take against you. I'm bringing this up because they make all types of claims and threats, and an ill-informed consumer will fall for it and pay them, when in some cases they really don't have to.

1. They can request that the account be closed. If it's in collections, more than likely this has happened all ready and in some cases, the debt has already been both charged and written off as a loss.

2. They can report the debt to the credit bureaus. This is quite damaging to a credit score and can drop it in excess of 80 points in some cases. This is their number one tactic to lure people into paying a debt.

3. They can sue you. Remember this. ANYONE CAN SUE YOU! The key thing is they have to WIN, which means you have to defend yourself. This is easier than it sounds, but you can find assistance by obtaining a free legal aid attorney, a pro bono attorney, taking advantage of a Free Consultation with an attorney that specializes in dealing with collection agencies or consumer rights; or signing up with Legal Shield and using one of their attorneys. I've had much success using the latter two. The main point I'm making is that before a debt collector can garnish your wages, levy your bank accounts, attach a lien to your asset, they have to win. And if you're proactive about it, you can prevent that from happening.

During the call, the collector will give you minor – and I do mean minor – details of the debt. They will ask you for payment arrangements to pay the account off in full. FULL? Yes, full. They will never, ever, ever inform you of any other payment arrangement first other than payment in full. It is not until you have been adamant about your inability to take care of the account that they will give you other options – payment arrangements to pay in full (this always 2nd); settle the account in full, meaning a one payment settlement; or settle the account via payment arrangements.

If you have not validated this debt – and I don't care if you recognize the creditor, the debt or the amount they are attempting to collect; you will not pay them. Notice I didn't say you *should* not pay them, I said you WILL NOT pay them until you have taken advantage of your 30 day right to request verification. Why? With the amount of fraud going on today, it is imperative to get all the details on the account in addition to proof of the relationship between the original company and the collector calling you to ensure that if you do decide to make arrangements with them you are paying the right company. In addition, most of the transferring, assigning and purchasing of debts is automated, completed online and in bulk. So....there is a big chance that this company does not have all of the documentation necessary to collect on this debt in the first place. Use this to your advantage; we'll discuss the validation letter and the process in detail a bit later.

During the phone call, you'll encounter 3 types of collectors: The Nice Guy, the Shaming Guy, and the Angry Guy.

The Nice Guy is just that, nice. This collector will be cordial, respectful, kind, considerate, empathetic, sympathetic and understanding. Don't fall for it. Their objective is simply to get your money and their bonus. The more they collect, the more they make, and the day goes by so much quicker if they can collect without being a butt to anyone. You can be nice as well, but remember your objective and their objective. You – get off the phone. Them – get your money. So, politely tell them that you aren't sure of too many of the details of the account, this isn't a good time right now, and if they can send you the details in writing that'll be great. Be sure to add that due to the nature of your work hours (or your schedule), you'd prefer to communicate with them in writing only. They will try to keep you on the phone, but don't fall for it. Only stay on long enough to provide them with your mailing address to send correspondence to and hang up. Some consumers will provide them with the wrong address. This is stupid. Remember, we're stacking violations and you can find them in that letter. Further, if they do decide to take legal action you want to receive the notifications. When you receive the dunning letter, review it, compare it to your records, if any, and send them a validation letter (I have a few templates available in the Appendix Section).

The Shaming Guy makes you feel like crap for not paying your debts. His objective is to make you feel ashamed, guilty, irresponsible, and overall bad about your current predicament! Believe it or not, attacking a consumer's character does work. People will make payment arrangements to prove that they are not a bad person. PULEEZ! Who is this person on the phone that you have to prove anything to them? I'll answer that, no one! Do not bother stooping to their level, it's a complete waste of your energy that can be applied to something more productive. Simply, tell them to only communicate with you in writing, mail you all of the documentation on the phone, confirm their address and get off the phone. I will say that the shaming guy will not be as polite about you getting off the phone. He will make threats about escalating your account with a manager, stressing that he doesn't want to take further collection activities and would like to take care of this today, or point out different activities that you've done recently and ask why you can't take care of your financial responsibilities. The nerve! The latter conversation will go something like this: *"I see you've recently applied for a home loan, you know that having all of your accounts resolved can greatly improve your chances of getting approved, right?"* Or, *"I see that you have recently traveled to Dubai, is that why you can't take care of this debt today?"*

Ignore. Ignore. Ignore. Be firm, tell them legally they have to send you written communication of the debt within 5 days, please do NOT call you anymore, only communicate in writing, make sure they have your correct address, and hang up.

The Angry Guy's main purpose is to scare you. He will make all types of claims, from threatening to sue you, arrest you, garnish your wages, take your house, your car, drain your bank accounts; etc. Please remember what I said earlier, they have to sue you AND win. A collector will only sue you if they feel they can win, or if the debt, your assets, or your income are worthy of the costs and their efforts. Most debts are not worth pursuing legal remedies. In regards to arresting you, debt collection is a civil issue, not criminal. In most cases the police will not get involved and you will not go to jail for failure to pay a debt. Thus, the angry guy's tactics are to merely freak you out into thinking that these things will take place. Further, the FDCPA forbids a collection agency from making threats that they do not and/or cannot carry out. Feel free to call him out on it. *"Don't you have to win a lawsuit and file a judgment claim to be able to garnish my wages?" "Are you making threats of legal action that you don't plan on following through with? You know that's illegal, right?"* Afterwards, do exactly as you did with the Shaming Guy; reduce communication to writing only, request for them to send all details regarding the debt in the mail, confirm your mailing address and get off the phone.

NOTE: In an attempt to locate you, a debt collector may obtain the contact information of your friends/family members and begin to contact them. This is legal. They cannot contact a family member over and over again about your debt, unless they feel they can obtain updated information on how to locate you, they cannot reveal any aspect of the debt to them, or inform them of any actions they plan to take to collect on your debt, this is a violation of the FDCPA. If this has happened, in your cease and desist letter make sure to include verbiage to stop all communication with 3rd parties.

To read more on what debt collectors can and cannot do, see Sections 805 – 808 of the FDCPA in the Appendix Section.

Debt Collectors – Cease & Desist Letter

Cease & Desist Letter

Remember when you were requesting that all communication regarding the debt be done in writing? Well, this is your LEGAL RIGHT! Yep, you do not have to speak with a debt collector over the phone ever again, unless YOU want to. This is based on the FDCPA §805 (c) (see Appendix). This means no more harassing phone calls, no more crazy threats, no more obnoxious, condescending, irritating collectors on your line – you are free. Bask in it ☺.

Make sure you don't take your cease and desist demand too far by telling a collector to stop all communication with you – writing _and_ telephone. This is so not wise. You want some form of communication so that you can be notified of their intention to pursue further collection activities; namely sue you.

Keep in mind, collection agencies aren't the only ones that know if you are worthy of being pursued for a judgment; you are too. If you're gainfully employed, have assets and the amount of the debt is higher than the costs to sue you; you're at risk. If you do not have a job, any assets, and/or your income is protected from creditors – social security, disability, unemployment, etc. (look up your state laws) – you are considered judgment proof. No one will be suing you _until_ your financial situation improves to where you are no longer protected.

Send a simple request to cease and desist all telephonic communication and to write only. I have a few sample letters in the Appendix Section for assistance.

Debt Collectors - Statute of Limitations

Statute of Limitations on Debt (SOL)

I mentioned 'suing you' as one of the primary methods of collecting a debt by a collection agency. Your state's statute of limitations has a lot to do with a collection agency's decision to go that route. The Statute of Limitations on Debt is the time frame that a company can sue you to enforce payment of a debt.

Your SOL is a powerful defense when dealing with collection agencies. Each state's SOL differs in regards to time frame, and in what conditions that time frame can restart the SOL clock to Day One.

There are also different limitations depending on the type of debt that you have.

> Example 1: In IL credit card debts are 5yrs, written contracts are 10yrs; if you are in collections for writing a bad check, the SOL is 3yrs; and if a creditor is pursuing you for something you bought from their store (furniture, appliances, etc., excluding credit card transaction; it's 4 yrs.

> Example 2: In NY credit card debt is generally 6yrs; for a department store credit card, it's 4 years; and even shorter for credit card issuers who's contracted statute of limitations is shorter than 6 years. For example; the _contracted statute of limitations_ is what you agreed to when you signed your contract. In most credit card agreements the bank will list whose state laws

they follow, for Discover, Chase and Bank of America, their SOLs are set for 3yrs. They will pursue you past those 3 years IF your state's statute of limitations is longer. In 2010, NY said "NO!" If your statute of limitations is 3, 4, or 5 years, then that's all you get, don't pursue our residents using our 6 year SOL as a basis. Good stuff right?!

Example 3: The Universal Commercial Code has set the statute of limitations for credit cards to 4 years; this could be a great defense if your state's statute of limitations is longer because the Universal Commercial Code can take precedence over state laws if argued correctly.

The statute of limitations is REALLY important and something you should look up immediately prior to contacting any creditor regarding a debt. Keep in mind:

A collection agency can still pursue you for payment on a debt they have purchased after the SOL has expired.

A collection agency *may* try to sue you, even though the debt is past your state's statute of limitations.

Yes, you read that correctly. It is up to YOU to bring up your statute of limitations as a defense, not the collection agency.

You can look up your statute of limitations on your state's Attorney General Website, or with a quick Google search. You'll want to see if your state has an

<u>affirmative defense</u> statute or a <u>claim-invalidating</u> statute.

Affirmative Defense: An affirmative defense statute allows a collection agency to pursue any collection activity against you that is past your state's SOL, except sue you. Suing a consumer for a debt that is past their SOL is a violation of the FDCPA. If a suit has been brought against you and it's past the SOL, you can present this information with as much proof as you have for a swift dismissal.

Claim-Invalidating: A claim-invalidating statute prevents a collection agency from taking *any action* to collect on a debt if it's past your state's SOL

Here is the site that I use to look up credit card agreements and the state's statute of limitations; both are good for 2 reasons – (A) You want to know which state's statute of limitations apply; (2) you want to know what fees you agreed to be added to the original balance if the account is now with a collection agency and additional fees and interest have been added:

<u>http://www.consumerfinance.gov/credit-cards/agreements/</u>

Always remember that a creditor will try to apply whatever state's statute that benefits them the most. If their contracted state is longer, they'll go with that, if the state you charged the account in is longer they'll go with that one, if you've moved and your new state's laws are longer, they'll go with that one. It is YOUR job to bring up the statute of limitation defense when disputing for validation, or during a legal defense.

Debt Collectors – Acknowledging the Debt

Acknowledgment of the Debt

One thing that can restart your SOL is acknowledgment of the debt. For this reason, a lot of financial experts will advise you to not speak with debt collectors over the phone in order to avoid acknowledging the debt and extending your state's statute of limitations. This will not happen.

The majority of the U.S. (44 states and the District of Columbia) require your acknowledgement to be in writing in order to restart or toll (stop) the statute of limitations. The other 6 states: Kentucky, Hawaii, Maryland, Pennsylvania, Rhode Island, and Tennessee; has specific guidelines as to what extent a verbal acknowledgment will be recognized as 'acknowledgment'. This is why it is so important to read your state's SOL guidelines.

Another thing that can restart the statute of limitations is making a payment – partial, or full. However, this isn't black or white either. Some states require a written agreement of the debt, regardless of a payment made or not. These states include: Arizona, California, Florida, Iowa, Kansas, Maine, Massachusetts, Michigan, Minnesota, Mississippi, Missouri, Nevada, New York, Texas, Virginia, West Virginia, and Wisconsin. Again, please read your state's statute for more information, and for the most up to date data.

If you review your state's guidelines and still have questions, feel free to contact your state's attorney general office, a local attorney (free consultation, of course), perform a Google search - sticking to reputable or government consumer advocacy websites - or visit your local Consumer Protection Office, you'll find a slew of goodies and free assistance there; (you can look this up at www.usa.gov and click on State, and then Consumer Protection Offices).

Debt Collectors - Validation

The Validation Process

Your 30 day right to dispute a debt is your request for validation.

The FDCPA isn't too detailed on what constitutes proper validation, so be sure to check your state collection laws to see if they expand on what is required for validation. Alabama, Texas and Massachusetts, for example, have some great additions to the FDCPA that collection agencies must provide.

You are also able to send a validation letter after the 30 days. Since dunning letters are not sent certified mail or any other method that tracks your receipt of it, you can send the validation letter 30 days after discovery of the debt. This can be a phone call, another letter or after seeing it on your credit report(s).
NOTE: If you fail to dispute the debt within 30 days, it does not automatically mean that the debt is valid. Per FDCPA Section 809 4(c): **The failure of a consumer to dispute the validity of a debt under this section may not be construed by any court as an admission of liability by the consumer.**"

Validation Defined

Validation, according to Black's Law Dictionary, is *"Assessing an action to determine it is complete, correct, implemented and delivering the correct outcome."*

In summary, validation is PROOF, physical documentation (or in some cases their audio recordings for 'quality assurance') that supports their claims regarding the debt in their systems.

You need those documents in order to check for accuracy, completeness, to ensure the paperwork justifies their claims, and that it meets all of the necessary requirements per state, federal and contractual law.

You can obtain this information by requesting it in a letter that is crafted during the 30 day right to dispute period. In your dispute, you will ask for documentation that supports their claims of being in ownership of the debt, proof of the debt itself, proof of the accuracy of the amount being collected, and proof of your obligation to pay them.

Let's review what you can ask for in your dispute letter.

Validation Letter

Here is what I typically request in my validation letters:

1. Identify the original creditor

2. A copy of the original contract with my original 'wet' signature; front and back.
   a. Some debts are obtained online, such as credit cards. As I mentioned previously, when we check the box and digitally sign agreeing that it can be used in place of our wet signature, this is legal and valid. Some will argue that because a document does not have our original signature on it, it is not valid. Again, once we

use the account, make payments on the account, a contract is formed based on the actions of both parties, this is often referred to as an implied contract. Make sure to request a copy of this form of contract as well, if applicable.

3. A copy of the contract between them and the original creditor.
   a. This can be an assignment agreement or a purchase agreement. If the debt was purchased from another collection agency, you want to have a copy of all the agreements starting from the original creditor to the current one. Yep, all of them.

4. Proof that they are licensed and bonded (if required) in your state
   a. If you live in a larger city, check your state collection laws to see if a collector must be licensed in both your state and your city.

5. A complete transaction history. This can be provided via invoices, an accounting ledger, or printouts of the full account history directly from the original creditors – NOT the collection agency's – system. You will need every charge, payment, interest rate, fees, etc. for the entire life of the account; from the moment it was opened until now.
   a. If the account is over 5 years old, creditors (not collection agency) are allowed to provide you with transaction history for the past 48 months.

6. Proof that debt is within your state's Statute of Limitations. Statute of limitation is the time, set

by each state that an entity has to sue you to collect on a debt. If the debt is past the statute of limitations, I wouldn't bother paying it, we'll discuss this a bit further later on.

7. Inquire if any judgments have been filed

8. Inquire if any insurance claims have been filed by the original creditors on the debt
9. Cease & Desist language to limit communication to writing only

10. Response within 30 days is requested.

Additional information you can request, but that can be found in the documents requested above as well:

- The name & address of the original creditor,
- The name of the alleged debtor (potentially you) on file
- The alleged account number
- The amount of the alleged debt
- Explain to me how you calculated this amount
- The date the debt became payable
- The date of the original charge off or the first date of delinquency
- The amount debt collector paid for the debt, if the debt was purchased

- Name & address of all persons, entities, associations or any other party having an interest in legal proceedings regarding the debt
- If a 3rd party debt collector, produce evidence that you are truly a 3rd party collector and have not purchased the debt and are really collecting in your name
- Produce notarized evidence from the original creditor that you are authorized to act for them

Why will you add this to the letter if it can be found in the documents you have requested already? Because the *"Debtor must phrase their request clearly to obtain the source of a debt and the amount a bad debt buyer paid for plaintiff's debt, how amount sought was calculated, where in issue a list of reports to credit bureaus, and documents conferring authority on defendant to collect debt"* (Coppola v. Arrow Financial Services, 2002). Further, there's no better way to get a point across than repetition.

You can add so much more to your list of requests, in addition to the ones you may find in your state law requirements. As long as it's within both state and federal law, or it is needed in order to prove the claims in connection with the collection attempts from the collection agency, ask away. I've included a few Validation Letters in the Appendix Section for your reference.

All communication with collection agencies should be documented and *underlined!* NEVER, EVER, EVER sign a validation letter or send any identification documents, such as your driver's license or social security card, or anything with that type of information on there. Why? Umm, you're asking them to provide you with documents that show you are responsible for the debt, which includes your signatures on documents, your social, your address, and other identification information, why make their job any easier and more importantly, why give them the information to potentially forge any documents? Has this happened before? Who knows, but considering how some debt collectors behave, I would not put it past them. Keep your signatures off the letters and do not attach any supporting identification documentation unless it shows the account has been satisfied.

You'll send the validation letter certified mail or first class mail with a signature confirmation/return receipt. This way you'll have documented proof of the receipt and the company representative that signed for it, if needed in the future. File it along with the dunning letter until you receive your response.

NOTE: Dunning letters come with fax numbers and email addresses marked specifically for disputes. I have had success sending them via fax and email as well, ensuring that detailed records are maintained.

I've Sent the Letter, Now What?

Aah, the hard part; waiting! In most letters we request a response within 30 days. However, the FDCPA does not specify when the debt collector has to respond. It does, however, disallow **_any_** collection activities to take place until the debt has been validated. This means, no reporting to the credit bureaus, no phone calls, no letters demanding payment, no lawsuits, etc.

From here the debt collector can send you the documentation they do have, which is usually limited; close the account; or sell the debt to recoup some of their investment.

If the collection agency sells the debt, you will need to request validation of the debt all over again. You could also let the new collection agency know that they have purchased an invalidated debt and to either give it back to the agency they purchased it from, or get ready to be sued for resuming collection activities on an invalidated debt.

Now, let's address some of the common responses that the collection agencies will send you.

Reviewing the Validation Responses

One thing to remember is that validation should come from the original creditor, not the collection agency's system. The collector needs to prove, via documentation, that a debt was owed to the original creditor, and that they are now collecting on their behalf via an assignment or because they've purchased the debt.

One of the most common responses my clients get is a billing statement. It can be one or even ten copies of past statements from the original creditor, somehow proving that my client owes the debt *and* is now obligated to pay them. Don't fall for this! A few billing statements doesn't prove anything, look at the 10 items I listed for validation above and ask yourself, was this provided to me? If the answer is no, they did not validate the debt properly and must cease all collection activities until they do.

Another common response is to send you a computer printout from their system showing the amount, interest and fees collected and the name and contact information of the original creditor.

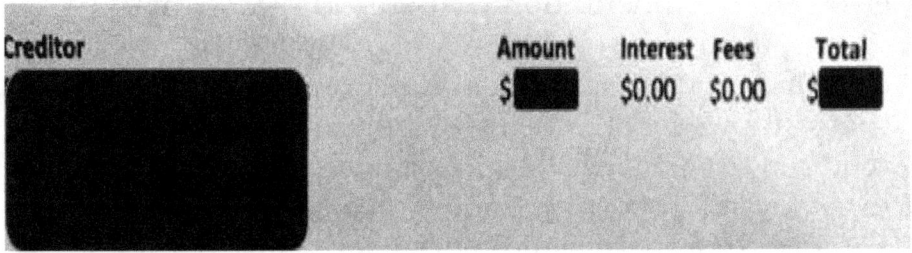

Creditor	Amount	Interest	Fees	Total
███████	$████	$0.00	$0.00	$████

This may meet *some* of the requirements of your validation request, but does it really give you proof of the debt *from the original creditor*? Remember validation is PROOF, does this show how the original creditor arrived at this balance? That the debt is not past your statute of limitations? That the collection agency is in ownership of the debt, that they are licensed/bonded to do business in your state? Absolutely not! You write them right back, tell them this is not validation, and until they are able to properly validate the debt per federal AND state regulations, all collection activities must cease and desist, including reporting any information to the credit bureaus.

Here is another popular response:

> X) We have completed our ~~investigation of your dispute~~. Our investi
> revealed that our original information was accurate. For your a
> convenience and ~~immediate credit, you may make~~ your debit or cre
> card payment at http://www.payaol.com.

Really? Of course you think your information is accurate! You want my money!!!! The validation process is _not_ for them to check their own records and miraculously determine they were right all along, it's to give YOU documentation that substantiates their claims. You write them back and ask for the documentation from the original creditor that proves that you owe what is being demanded and that you are required to pay them. Make sure to state that they are to remove all reporting from your credit files until they are able to properly validate the debt per federal and state guidelines. Another tactic that some collection agencies will use is to get you to send them documentation to 'speed matters up' or to 'help them' resolve your dispute in a timely fashion, or they act downright confused. DON'T FALL FOR THIS.

Remember any information you provide them – over the phone, in writing or any supporting documentation – will be used against you so that they can collect on the debt. Now, if you have proof that you paid that debt, then obviously send that in, but otherwise, any documentation they require should come from the original creditor, not you.
Here are some examples:

We understand that you are disputing the accuracy of our records concerning the above referenced account. After reviewing the information you provided, as well as our account notes, and information provided by the previous credito we are unable to determine the nature of your dispute, and consequently deny that our records are inaccurate. We wi closing our investigation of your dispute and resuming regular collection activities as allowed by the Texas Finance Co and/or the Fair Credit Reporting Act.

In response to your dispute, we have requested that the three major credit bureaus change the status of this accoun "Disputed". Your credit report will not be updated if the federal reporting period has expired.

If you still believe the account information is inaccurate, please provide an explanation of why you believe it is inaccu along with any documentation you have supporting this explanation. Upon receipt of this new information we will be happy to reinvestigate our records.

If you have additional documentation or information related to your dispute, please send it to:

The purpose of this letter is to advise you that you did not provide sufficient information to investiga dispute of the credit reporting of your above-referenced account pursuant to the Fair Credit Reporti

We understand that you are disputing the accuracy of our records concerning the above referenced After reviewing the information you provided, as well as our account notes, and information provide previous creditor, we are unable to determine the nature of your dispute, and consequently deny tha records are inaccurate.

In order to further investigate your dispute, we need additional information to identify the basis of yo including a complete explanation of your dispute would be helpful. Further, copies of any document may have to support your dispute. In the interim, we have requested that the three major credit bur change the status of this account to "Disputed".

Examples of documentation we need or which would be helpful include the following:

Paid in Full or Account Settled: a) a copy of the front and back of payment instrument with copy settlement offer or statement showing balance and account number; b) a copy of paid in full or settl letter showing account number.

Fraud or Identity Theft: a) a copy of a police report; b) Federal Trade Commission Fraud Affidavit been filled out (which can be obtained at www.ftc.gov/idtheft); or c) notarized fraud affidavit.

Now, if you look closely at the document above you will see that they have updated the account on your credit report as 'disputed'. This is allowed as per the Fair Credit Reporting Act, but it does not mean you should let it remain there if the account has not been properly validated. Dispute the collection with the credit bureaus requesting deletion based on it being an unverifiable account.

Another 'response' is to state that the account is accurate and to immediately offer a settlement to resolve the account. If you recall, FULL PAYMENT is the ultimate goal. If they offer a settlement right out of the gate, something is amiss. Either they have no proof of the debt or it's past the statute of limitations, or very close to it.

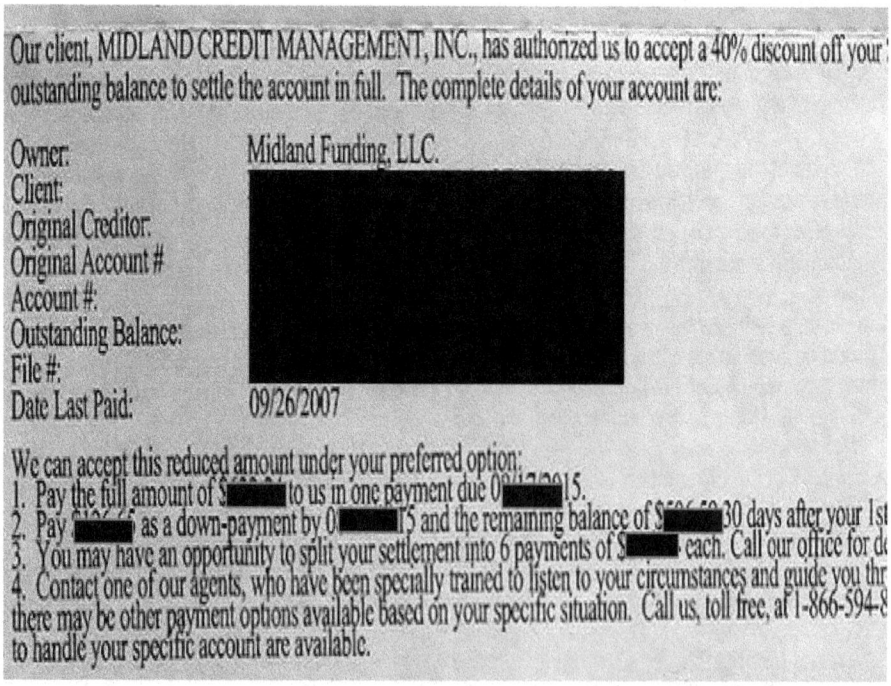

Our client, MIDLAND CREDIT MANAGEMENT, INC., has authorized us to accept a 40% discount off your outstanding balance to settle the account in full. The complete details of your account are:

Owner: Midland Funding, LLC.
Client:
Original Creditor:
Original Account #
Account #:
Outstanding Balance:
File #:
Date Last Paid: 09/26/2007

We can accept this reduced amount under your preferred option:
1. Pay the full amount of $████ to us in one payment due 0███2015.
2. Pay $███ as a down-payment by 0████T5 and the remaining balance of $██████30 days after your 1st
3. You may have an opportunity to split your settlement into 6 payments of $███ each. Call our office for d
4. Contact one of our agents, who have been specially trained to listen to your circumstances and guide you thr
there may be other payment options available based on your specific situation. Call us, toll free, at 1-866-594-8
to handle your specific account are available.

The first thing you want to look at is the "Date Last Paid" date. This particular letter was received in 2015 and the debt was last paid in 2007. What does that tell you? (A) It's past federal reporting limitations, all debts from 2007 should have been deleted in 2014 from your credit reports. (B) Depending on the state and the type of debt; it's the statute of limitations; or pretty darn close.

For this particular client, I wrote a full cease and desist letter, stating that the debt is past her state's statute of limitations, no proof of validation was furnished to her, and thus it's an invalidated debt, and to please cease and desist all communication, both in writing and over the phone.

If the Date Last Paid was within her SOL, I would demand true validation, ensuring documents are from the original creditor, and for them to cease all collection activities until it is provided.

Another common tactic is to misrepresent case laws. By quoting a case, they can easily deceive consumers who are not well versed in consumer laws. Here's an extremely popular quote regarding Chaudhry v. Gallerizzo (1998): *"..verification of a debt involves nothing more than the debt collector confirming in writing that the amount being demanded is what the creditor is claiming is owed; the debt collector is not required to keep detailed files of the debt. There is no concomitant obligation to forward copies of bills or other detailed evidence of the debt."*

Umm, we asked for _validation_, right? Further, the verification or validation of the debt was not in question with this lawsuit; legal fees were. So, if you receive this, follow the same pattern as above. Call them out on their inability to validate the debt, inform them that this case did not address validation of a debt, and if they cannot provide you with proper validation, you will consider it unverifiable and all collection activity and credit reporting must cease and desist immediately.

Sending irrelevant documents posed as legal proof is another ploy. When a consumer receives a letter similar to the one below they become confused and are deceived into thinking the debt is legit. Remember, validation comes from the original creditor, not the collection agency. An affidavit of ownership is nothing more than a debt collector stating "Yes, I own this debt now". Really? Don't fall for this.

AFFIDAVIT OF OWNERSHIP AND SALE OF CLAIM

State of ███████

City of ██████ ss.

I, the undersigned, ███████████████ , Administrative Manager, for ██████████████
Associates, LLC hereby depose, affirm and state, to the best of my understanding and belief

1. I am an authorized employee of ██████████████████████████ ("Account Assignee")
which is doing business at ████████████████████████████████.
Virginia, and I am authorized to make the statements, representations and averments herein.

2. According to the account records provided to the Account Assignee by Sears ("Account
███████████████ from ██████████ ("Debtor") to the Account Seller the

66

Sometimes a collector will not respond at all. Believe it or not, some will continue to report negative information to your credit files each month, still send you demand letters and call you as if you never sent them a thing. This is why you send your dispute with a signature confirmation. That way, when they report anything, call or mail anything you have proof that a representative received your request, and violated the FDCPA by continuing collection activities anyway. And for the agencies that didn't respond to you and stopped communicating with you all together? They're following the law. No response does not always equal a bad thing. Although we requested a response within 30 days, the FDCPA does not place sanctions on collection agency if they fail to respond within that time frame. They do require, however, that a collection agency stop all collection activities until they validate the debt.

Until this happens, you can send a dispute letter to the credit bureaus and request a deletion of the unverifiable collection account reporting, the collector cannot verify the debt because they have failed to provide validation per the FDCPA. You now have a deletion☺. If the bureaus respond that the account has been verified, I'd file a complaint on both the bureaus and the collection agency because obviously either the bureau is lying or the collection agency is performing illegal collection activities on your invalidated account. Your complaint will be filed with the Consumer Financial Protection Bureau, the Better Business Bureau, and/or your state's Attorney General's Office.

The ultimate goal is to receive this:

Keep in mind, most collection accounts will require more than one round of disputes. This means, you will have to write more than one letter in order to get a resolution, in some cases up to three to four letters.

Remember, a large part of a debt collector's job is to be persistent; after all, a payment on your account is the key to their next bonus check. There are only a few reasons a debt collector will stop pursuing you for payment:

- You have died with no estate/no one handling your debts
- You have filed bankruptcy
- Your debt is past the statute of limitations (in some states)
- You are represented by an attorney
- You are a victim of identity theft and can prove it

- Your income is protected as 'collection/judgment proof' (check state laws)
- They've sold your account
- The account cannot be verified/validated

Therefore, you need to be just as persistent. Keep stellar records, track phone calls, conversations and violations; be vigilant!

The 'Other' Side of Validation

According to a CFPB report, collection agencies only collect on 21% of the debts they purchase. That means that 79% of their debts prove to be uncollectible.

The best way to ensure that they collect on that 21% is to focus on the debts that are easy to collect and that will bring in the most profit. If you are a part of that 79% and you send a validation letter, you are putting a big "NOTICE ME" sign on your file and it can lead to more aggressive collection activity that never would have been performed in the first place.

Does that mean you should not send a validation letter? Of course not. It is your right to ensure that the debts that are placed with collection agencies are legit.

However, if a collection agency is able to obtain all of the documentation necessary to prove your debt, they may use every action they can to collect on it, including suing you.

Older debts don't pose too much of a threat, but newer debts do. On August 4, 2014, the Office of the Comptroller of the Currency mandated new requirements that must be abided by when selling debts to collection agencies.

These include:

- A copy of the signed contract or supporting documentation that proves the consumer's responsibility to pay the debts.

- Copies of all, or the past year's account statements (whichever is less).

- All account numbers used by the bank that are tied to the debt being purchased.

- A full accounting of the amount(s) being collected on - loan principal, interest, and fees.

- The name of the issuing bank/store name.

- The date of the debtor's last payment, date the account became delinquency, the amount owed, source of previous payments

- Records pertaining to disputes, fraud claims, and collection efforts prior to the sale.

- Consumer's name, address, social security number.

As you can see these meet most of the requirements for proper validation. Again, does this mean you should not request validation? NO! Violations will still occur. Further, just because they can meet the minimum requirements for federal validation; doesn't mean they can meet some of the requirements for state validation. And it is your consumer right! Just make sure it is done strategically. If you receive a letter from the original creditor, for example, notifying you of the sale of your account to a collection agency prior to them mailing out your dunning letter, I'd start getting a plan of action together. Once you send them a validation letter *and* they provide everything that you ask for, then what are you going to do?

This is why I provided you with this information. In the past, very few collectors were able to fully validate a debt, because banks were not required to provide them with the supporting documentation that I listed above. I personally have still not had a collection agency be able to fully validate a debt, but that could very well change. Now, more than ever, it is important that you have a Plan B in place from the very beginning.

Debt Collectors – Plan B

Your Plan B

Stacking violations is still the most effective way to deal with collection agencies. The documentation required to sell a debt may have changed, but the tactics to collect on the debt has not. Stacking violations is your Plan A. KNOW YOUR RIGHTS!!!

Some of my clients are only concerned with the reporting of the collection on their credit reports, and if that's the case, once you have the documentation supporting the collection account, fact check it against what is reported on your credit report to ensure accuracy. As a professional, I like to work on permanently resolving the debt; simply removing it from your credit report is a credit scoring solution; not a debt destroying solution.

Your Plan B depends on you and the financial resources you have available.

Actually paying a collection agency after they have validated a debt is an option. Most experts will tell you never to pay a debt collector under any circumstances; however, that is strictly a personal decision and I let my clients call it. I personally have had great success settling newer collection accounts in exchange for a deletion from my client's credit reports. Newer collections can drop a credit score over 80 points; by removing the collection from the report as if it never reported, a credit score will soar quite significantly. I am all for paying newer collection accounts that have been validated in order to rid my clients of the headache permanently. Why? We can spend time disputing back and forth, or we can come up with a plan to get rid of the debt permanently in less than 30 days. If my clients have the money, they are completely on board for the latter option.

In my experience, if you decide to pay a newer validated collection account, settling the account in full works best. Collection agencies are all about money. You can get quite a reduction off the original amount by offering a full settlement rather than splitting the payment up into installments. How much you can get reduced from the full balance depends on your negotiation skills. They'll shoot high; you'll shoot low; and you'll both end up settling in between. Just make sure the amount you agree on truly works in your favor. You shouldn't have to miss your mortgage/rent or car payment in order to pay a debt collector. Don't be afraid to walk away from negotiations if you don't get what you want. The last thing a collector wants to hear is you hanging up the phone when you were so close to making a payment. Don't sound desperate or urgent, you will lose all ground if you do that. Be firm, matter of fact, and again walk away if you have to; they'll call back.

As far as removing the account from your credit report, that will need to be negotiated as well. With the exception of medical collections, the answer will always be no. They'll state the original creditor will not allow them to do that, the FCRA requires them to only report accurate information, it is against their policy, etc. So, how do you get them to do it? You negotiate prior to paying them. The only item that is required to report on any consumer's credit report is child support; everything else is voluntary. Further, you're not asking them to 'report' an inaccurate account, you're asking them to remove it completely, that's different; and as far as their policy goes; who cares? You want the deletion! Paying in full or settling in full works best. Nothing 'speaks' better than a stack full of cash closing out the account completely. Record the conversation stating they'll delete the account or get it in writing via an email or formal letter faxed/mailed over to you.

If the debt has been assigned rather than sold; paying the original creditor may be an option. Most will refuse to speak with you regarding the account once they've hired a collection agency. I simply inform my clients to write a letter refusing to do business with the collection agency and that they'll only speak with the original creditor to make payment arrangements. A similar letter is sent to the original creditor letting them know we are willing to make payment arrangements on the account, but will only work with them. I follow up with a phone call upon receipt of the letter (send it with signature confirmation so that you know when they receive it) and make arrangements for payment. If you go this route, make sure they pull the account from the collection agency.

Ultimately, a paid collection looks better than an unpaid collection. Will the effects of a collection go away simply because you paid it? Absolutely not. However, when lenders are approving you for a home or some other form of credit, they'd like to see a paid collection account rather than an unpaid one.
If you are successful in settling the account, make sure you get all of the terms in writing, making sure they specify that they will forfeit their rights to sell or collect on the balance.

Doing nothing is also an option. Remember, only 21% of collection accounts are collected on. If you are 'judgment proof', are incapable of paying the account off right now, and can't make arrangements to take care of the debt no matter how much they call or write; doing nothing is an option. Just make sure you communicate this and open and file every single piece of correspondence they mail you. If they feel you are a part of their 21%; they will try to sue you. Keep in mind, collection agencies pursue less than 8% of their accounts for litigation.

Debt Collectors - Complaints

Where to Send Complaints

I only send complaints when my client is well protected. This means the violations are well documented and solid, the refusal to comply with their rights are recorded or documented, and making sure that filing a complaint will not expose them to more aggressive collection activities.

CFPB

The Consumer Financial Protection Bureau acts as the consumer's 'watchdog'. They protect consumers against shady practices by companies in the financial industry. They pretty much enforce the consumer rights laws that are already in place and write additional rules in order to restrict any unfair or abusive practices. They also take complaints and monitor financial markets in order to identify and prevent new risks that could negatively impact the consumer.

The CFPB monitors third party debt collectors (assigned the debt), debt purchasers (bought the debt) and debt attorneys (suing to collect the debt). When a violation has occurred, a complaint with the CFPB can be filed to enforce compliance. They are a valuable tool to utilize when dealing with violations.

BBB

Filing a complaint with the BBB is a great way to get results. If you are disputing any item on your credit report that is truly inaccurate, incomplete or unverifiable, a BBB complaint can get you in communication with a high-level representative directly with the company. I use this method for companies that refuse to validate after 3 attempts, violate my consumer rights, ignore my attempts to resolve the account (I want to settle, they want full payment), and when I want to rouse 'noise' because they are being unreasonable to deal with.

FTC (FDCPA VIOLATIONS)

I will only file a Fair Trade Commission complaint when I have stacked enough well-documented violations to make a difference. This is a phenomenal method of getting rid of debts completely (if they are uncollectible or the debt is lower than the amount of the collections) or to get the upper hand.

SAG

I love my state Attorney General's Office! I utilize them when a collector is not licensed in my client's state, when they (or credit bureaus) violate their state or federal consumer rights, or when a collector (or company) refuses to accept my client's phone calls (yes, this happens). A complaint can be made in one of two ways:

1. Filing a complaint directly with the SAG office
2. Filing a complaint in order to have them intervene on my client's behalf.
    a. Example: My client had a creditor that refused to speak with them once they transferred their account over to a collection agency. The debt was reporting

in error because the equipment had been returned. A quick call to the SAG and they called an executive within the company to discuss the account on my client's behalf. Needless to say, the collection was deleted and an apology letter was issued to my client. Gotta love it ☺.

ACA

For complaints about a collection agency's ethical conduct, I go to the American Collectors Association. If the collection agency is a part of this association, they are bound by the moral and ethical industry standards that they must abide by in order to remain a member. I've found this to be very useful in getting the Angry Guy or Shaming Guy collector to sing another tune. No matter what type of debtor a collection agency encounters, it is up to them to remain professional at all times.

These are my top five companies that I've had success with over the past 10 years. They are extremely effective in getting satisfactory results.

Most Common Violations

FTC/FDCPA – We've covered this extensively, and I have a full text of the Act in the Appendix Section.

Fair Credit Reporting Act – If an account is unverifiable and they continue to report it on your credit report, this is a violation. If they report to your credit report during the validation period, this is a violation. If they report during your 30 day right to dispute period, this is a violation.

Gramm-Leach-Bliley Act – The GLBA requires financial institutions to create and inform consumers about how they will use their non-public personal information. If this notice is received during your 30 day right to dispute, this is a violation.

Telephone Consumer Protection Act – The TCPA forbids autodialed or prerecorded non-emergency calls to cell phone numbers unless the call is made with "the prior express consent of the called party." Consent can be given to the original creditor and assigned with the debt to the 3rd party debt collector. However, consent has to be given when a telephone number is provided while discussing the debt; not while discussing anything else on the account, such as services.

Bankruptcy Automatic Stay – If a collection agency pursues collection activities after you have filed bankruptcy – yes, filed, not completed/discharged – they have violated the automatic stay and could face a fine. The bankruptcy court will need to be notified, and depending on how aggressive collection activities were, it may be beneficial to file a lawsuit.

HIPAA – The Health Insurance Portability & Accountability Act sets privacy rules regarding a patient's protected health information.   If you request validation and the documents provided reveal too much about your medical condition, illness or treatment, there's a chance that a HIPAA violation has occurred, and a complaint can be filed.

There may be more violations that have occurred, if my clients have gathered a significant amount of violations and haven't gotten anywhere in regards to negotiations, or the collection agency has decided to file a lawsuit despite the fact that the account has not been properly validated or to scare my client into settling the account in lieu of a lawsuit; we get that collection file out, go to one of my attorneys in my network and put that debt to rest. In most cases, my client ends up with money in their pockets. That's the power of the 'stacking violations' method!

Summary of My 10 Proven Steps

Summary of Steps

Step One: Google the Company. You always want to know who you're up against. Are they known to violate FDCPA guidelines? Are they known to sue at the drop of a hat? Are they known to settle right away? Are they known to remove items from credit reports with payment? All of this information can be found on various credit forums such as myfico.com, creditboards.com, creditinfocenter.com, debt attorney blogs, consumer rights attorney blogs.

Step Two: Check Your state's SOL. If it's a newer collection, they will have more leverage and you may need to settle the account if they can properly validate the debt (especially if it was assigned). If it's past or very near your SOL you have the upper hand, and the ability to walk away completely. Simply send a letter pointing out the debt is past SOL and to cease and desist all communications with you. I've listed links to each state's SOL in the Appendix Section.

Step Three: Review your Federal and State Collection Laws. An educated consumer is a powerful consumer!

Step Four: What your next step should be depends on how you became aware of the collection item.

> Via Your Credit Report – Were you notified of the debt via a dunning letter? If not, no collection activity should take place prior to notifying you of your 30 day right to dispute. Is the account reporting correctly? Is the balance correct? The dates? The status? Send a verification letter

disputing whatever aspect of the account is reporting inaccurately for deletion. Wait 30-45 days for a response.

If you're not sure if any of the information is reporting inaccurately, send a validation dispute letter using the address listed on your credit report. If you cannot find the address on the credit report, Google the company, they will typically list their address or fax number to send a validation letter to on their website. If that fails, the BBB website has pretty accurate info. Wait 30-45 days for a response.

TIP: Over 70% of the time I send the validation letter first, and send a verification letter to the credit bureaus 3-5 days afterwards. Collection Agencies cannot verify a debt once they receive your request for validation letter. Therefore, if the credit bureaus 'verify' the account, one of them violated your consumer rights – the collection agency or the credit bureaus for failing to conduct a reasonable investigation.

Via a Telephone Call – Inform them to send the details of the debt in writing, do not admit to anything over the phone, do not answer any questions regarding knowledge of the debt, your income, employment or payment arrangements regarding the debt. Provide them with your name, address, and request that they send you everything in writing. Record any violations that may occur, heck, even record the phone call if you can! If you continue to get phone calls after you request that they send the details in writing, create a call log to record how many times they called you. Follow the instructions detailed above. Your main objective is to get it in writing.

Via a Dunning Letter – Look over the account in detail, check for violations as described above. Send a validation dispute letter. Wait 30-45 days for a response.

Step Five: Review response using the information above. Keep a running tally of any possible violations. Was full validation provided *by the original creditor?* Create your next plan of action using the information provided in this guide. Should you send another letter giving them a second attempt at validating the account? Should you send a letter telling them to cease and desist all communications and collection activities until the account has been validated according to federal and state regulations? Should you send a dispute letter to the credit bureaus to get rid of the account? Should you send a letter to the original creditor to see if they have any information regarding the account? Repeat, if necessary, in case they send you partial proof of the debt again.

Keep Plan B in mind, especially if it's a newer account or if it has been fully validated, such as in the case of assigned debts. If you decide to pay, examine the amount owed to ensure it's accurate, determine the amount you'll pay and negotiate based on that, get payment arrangements in writing (fax/email/mail) prior to payment.

Step Six: If violations have racked up, apply for local credit and get proof of denial or proof of less than more favorable terms due to the collection agency's reporting. Courts have ruled that consumers must prove actual harm resulting from inaccurate reporting. Prove it. Again, I would only do this if the violations have racked up and are now lawsuit worthy. This will provide you with more damages (more money) to solidify your case. You want a local lender!!! When/if it goes to court; a local lender can be easily subpoenaed.

Step Seven: Send collection agency (and original creditor if assigned and/or credit bureaus) a letter detailing the violations – federal and state – that have occurred, in addition to punitive and actual damages as well. State your case and what you want – deletion of account and inquiries from credit reports, an affidavit from a company executive that all personal information and records pertaining to the debt have been removed from their files. Wait 30 days for a response.

Step Eight: File a lawsuit in small claims court if response is not satisfactory and you have a solid case (attorney will tell you if it's a viable case, if you've done well keeping solid records you'll be fine).

Step Nine: File a lawsuit against the bureaus as well if they continue to report the debt after you have notified them it could not be verified/validated.

Step Ten: Settle the court case outside of court if the deal is good; if not go to court.

Conclusion

Conclusion

I hope the information and strategies provided in this guide are beneficial to you and that it helps you to achieve your ultimate goal of great credit and finances. For long-term results, I advise to aggressively practice good money and credit management skills; they can save you hundreds of thousands of dollars during your lifetime.

Stop Hiding! 10 Proven Strategies for Facing Debt Collectors Head One! is the 1st title released in the "Credit Makes $ense Series". This and future titles are designed to be short, to-the-point, and informative guides, whose tips and strategies can be immediately implemented to jumpstart your journey to financial health.

Thank you so much for taking the time to purchase and read my book, I truly appreciate it! I welcome any feedback and positive reviews so that I can continue to create content that is impactful and beneficial to you.

For exclusive tips, tricks and strategies on how to Destroy Your Debts, Grow Your Money, and Soar Your Credit Scores; **subscribe to my email list right away at <u>www.mnhcreditsolutions.com</u>**. My Credit Transformation Services, Online Courses, Workshops, Webinars, and Products will be listed there as well.

Feel free to get 'social' with me on one or all of my social media platforms, I've listed them below for your convenience. I look forward to seeing with you there!

Facebook:	www.facebook.com/MNHCreditSolutions
YouTube/: Google+	Credit Makes $ense w/The Frugal CrediTnista
Twitter:	www.twitter.com/FrglCrediTnista
Periscope:	www.periscope.tv/FrglCrediTnista
Instagram:	www.instagram.com/TheFrugalCrediTnista

Thanks again!!!

~ Netiva

Appendix – Dispute Letters

Appendix – Collection Dispute Letters

Cease & Desist Letters – Sent to collection agencies to stop them from calling you. I have listed 2, one to stop them from calling, but permitting them to write – this is best for debts that are within your state's statute of limitations – and the one that prevents them from calling or writing you. The latter is best for debts that are past your state's statute of limitations or that you are attaching documentation that proves the account was satisfied by either paying the original creditor, another collection agency, or via a bankruptcy discharge.

Cease & Desist Letter – One

[Date]

Creditor Name   *****SENT VIA
CERTIFIED MAIL*****
City, State, Zip

Reference Number:

RE: REQUEST FOR CEASING PHONE CALLS

Dear [name]:

I am requesting, in writing, that no telephone contact be made by your company, and/or your attorneys to my home, my cell phone, my place of employment, any friends, acquaintances, or family members.

If your offices attempt telephone communication with me or people I may work for or know, it will be considered harassment and I will have no choice but to file suit. All communications with me MUST be done in writing and sent to the address noted in this letter.

Under 15 USCA 1692 c of the Fair Debt Collection Practices Act, this is my formal notice for you to cease all telephone calls except for those permitted by federal law. I am not cutting off communication with your company but rather reduce all communication to writing.

Sincerely,

DO NOT SIGN

NAME
Address
City, State, Zip

Cease & Desist Letter – Two

[Date]

Creditor Name   *****SENT VIA CERTIFIED
MAIL*****
City, State, Zip

Reference Number:

Dear [name]:

You are hereby notified to immediately terminate any contact with me, or any members of my family or household or employer/place of business, regarding any matter concerning the collection of the alleged debt(s) you are attempting to collect. This notice shall include, but is not limited to written correspondence, as well as telephone communication.

This is a formal notice to <u>cease any communication</u> with me pursuant to FDCPA §1692c.

Please note that my current address is listed above. Any contact with a neighbor or other person will not be "locator" information, but grounds for legal action against you.

I do not admit or deny liability on the debt. I just want you to stop contacting me.

I intend to keep a log of any contacts you make with me after you receive this letter. I am aware that further communications by you will make you liable for $1,000.00 per communication, plus actual damages and attorney fees.

You may contact me by mail to tell me that you are ceasing communications, as allowed by federal law.

Sincerely,

NAME
Address

Cease Communication – Can't Pay; I typically send this when my client's income is 'Judgment Proof' or the debt has been fully validated by the original creditor and my client simply can't pay it.

[Date]

Creditor Name   *****SENT VIA CERTIFIED
MAIL*****
City, State, Zip

Reference Number:

Dear [name]:

I have received numerous telephone calls and letters from your company regarding a debt you are attempting to collect. At this time I am not able to pay due to (**insert reason: unemployment, under-employment; disability or some other judgment proof income {check state}**). This is not an acknowledgement of the debt, but simply a request to stop any and all communication with me, both in writing and over the phone, regarding it.

I was told the FDCPA allows me to request this and that you can only contact me again if my account status has changed or if you intend to file a lawsuit.

If I am able to work out payment arrangements in the near future I will contact your offices. As of right now, this is not the case.

Sincerely,

NAME
Address
City, State, Zip

Cease & Desist Letter – Refuse to do Business with You. I've used this for debts that have been assigned only. Some of my colleagues have used this for debts that have been purchased, which you can try at your own discretion.

[Date]

Creditor Name   *****SENT VIA CERTIFIED
MAIL*****
City, State, Zip

Reference Number:

Dear [name]:

I received your letter regarding an alleged debt. I decline to do business with your company. Unless you can present your lawful authority or a written agreement between me and you within 20 days, you cannot force me to do business with you. If you injure me in any way in an attempt to collect on this alleged debt, including placing an inquiry on my credit report or reporting any information to the credit reporting agencies, I will consider it attempted extortion and will have no choice but to act accordingly.

Sincerely,

Name

Cease & Desist Letter – Past SOL

[Date]

Creditor Name   *****SENT VIA CERTIFIED
MAIL*****
City, State, Zip

Reference Number:

Dear [name]:

I received your letter (if phone call adjust) concerning the above referenced account. Please consider this notification of my formal dispute; I do not owe this debt.

I have checked with my State's Attorney General's Office and have discovered that this debt is past (Insert State)'s statute of limitations, and payment cannot be enforced through our court system.

Therefore, I consider this matter closed and demand that all further contact by phone or mail from you, or anyone affiliated with your company, cease and desist. This includes any calls to my cell phone, work phone, mailing address, or any other medium.

If any of your records contradict the information above, please forward that information to me for my review, along with proof of your right to collect on this debt, a detailed account history of every transaction performed on the account from open to close, and any evidence that proves this debt is truly owed by me within 30 days.

Lacking this evidence, this debt is unverifiable and all collection activity must stop, including reporting any information to my credit reports.

Regards,

Name

Validation Letter – Simple

Date

Your Name
Address
City, State Zip

Debt Collector's Name
Address
City, State Zip

Re: Reference Number

Dear Debt Collector:

This letter is sent in response to <phone call/letter> received by you on <date>. I am requesting that you provide validation of this debt.

If you do not comply with this request, I will immediately file a complaint with the Federal Trade Commission and the [your state here] Attorney General's office. Civil and criminal claims will be pursued.

Sincerely,

Your Name

Validation Letter – Standard Letter you'll find many places online

Your Name
Your Address

Collector's Name
Collector's Address

Reference Number:

Dear {insert name of collector or company},

I am writing in response to your (letter or phone call) dated {insert date}, (copy enclosed) because I do not believe that I owe what you say I owe.

This is the first I've heard from you, or any other company on this matter therefore, in accordance with Section 809 - Validating Debts of the Fair Debt Collection Practices Act, I respectfully request that you provide me, in writing, the following:

- What the money you say I owe is for;
- Explain and show me how you calculated what you say I owe;
- Provide me with copies of any papers that show I agreed to pay what you
  say I owe; I want copies of the contract front and back
- Identify the original creditor;
- Provide a verification or copy of any judgment (if applicable);
- Show me that you are licensed in my state, and provide me with your license numbers (if applicable).

Be advised that I am fully aware of my rights under the Fair Debt Collection Practices Act and the Fair Credit Reporting Act. For instance, I know that:

- You cannot add interest or fees except those allowed by the original contract and state law.

- You do not have to respond to this dispute except to tell me that you either intend to cease your collection efforts or to pursue other legal means of collecting this debt.
- Should you pursue a judgment without validating this debt, I will inform the judge and your case will be dismissed based on your failure to follow the FDCPA.
- Any attempt to collect this debt without validating it, violates the FDCPA. Be advised that I intend to record all phone calls, keep all correspondence and will not hesitate to report violations to my State Attorney General, the Federal Trade Commission and the Better Business Bureau.

I have disputed this debt; therefore, until validated you know your information concerning this debt is inaccurate. Thus, if you have already reported this debt to any credit-reporting agency (CRA) or Credit Bureau (CB) then, you must immediately inform them this debt is in dispute. Reporting information that you know to be inaccurate or failing to report information correctly violates the FCRA § 1681s-2.

If you do NOT own the rights to collect this debt, I demand that you immediately send a copy of this dispute letter to the original creditor that you say I owe money too so they are also aware of my dispute with this debt.

Finally, in accordance with section 805(c) - Ceasing Collections, of the Fair Debt Collection Act, do not contact me about this or any other matter, except by official mail and then only to advise me that your debt collection efforts are being terminated or that you are taking specific actions allowed by law.

NEVER EVER EVER SIGN, PRINT ONLY!!!
Your Printed Name

Validation Letter – Detailed, can be tailored to your specific needs

Date

Your Name
Your Address

Collector's Name
Collector's Address

To Whom It May Concern,

I am sending this letter to you in response to a notice I received from you on (date of letter), (adjust if you found out about them by reviewing your credit report). Be advised this is not a refusal to pay, but a notice that your claim is disputed and validation is requested.

This is NOT a request for "verification" or proof of my mailing address, but a request for VALIDATION made pursuant to 15 USC 1692g Sec. 809 (b) of the FDCPA. I respectfully request that your offices provide me with competent evidence that I have any legal obligation to pay you.

At this time I will also inform you that if your offices have or continue to report invalidated information to any of the three major credit bureaus (Equifax, Experian, TransUnion), this action might constitute fraud under both federal and state laws. Due to this fact, if any negative mark is found or continues to report on any of my credit reports by your company or the company you represent, I will not hesitate in bringing legal action against you and your client for the following:

Violation of the Fair Debt Collection Practices Act
Defamation of Character

I am sure your legal staff will agree that non-compliance with this request could put your company in serious legal trouble with the FTC and other state or federal agencies.

If your offices are able to provide the proper documentation as requested in the following declaration, I will require 30 days to investigate this information and during such time all collection activity must cease and desist. Also, during this validation period, if any action is taken which could be considered detrimental to any of my credit reports, I will consult with legal counsel for suit. This includes any listing of any information to a credit-reporting repository that could be inaccurate or invalidated. If your offices fail to respond to this validation request within 30 days from the date of your receipt, all references to this account must be deleted and completely removed from my credit file and a copy of such deletion request shall be sent to me immediately.

It would be advisable that you and your client assure that your records are in order before I am forced to take legal action.

(2nd Page Follows)

CREDITOR/DEBT COLLECTOR DECLARATION

Please provide the following:

• Agreement with your client that grants you the authority to collect on this alleged debt.
• Agreement that bears the signature of the alleged debtor wherein he/she agreed to pay the creditor.
• Any insurance claims been made by any creditor regarding this account.
• Any judgments obtained by any creditor regarding this account.
• Name and address of alleged creditor.
• Name on file of alleged debtor.
• Alleged account number.
• Address on file for alleged debtor.
• Amount of alleged debt.
• Date this alleged debt became payable.
• Date of original charge off or delinquency.
• Verification that this debt was assigned or sold to collector.
• Complete accounting of alleged debt.
• Commission for debt collector if collection efforts are successful.

Please provide the name and address of the bonding agent for Client Services, Inc in
case legal action becomes necessary.

Your claim cannot and WILL NOT be considered if any portion of the above is not completed and returned with copies of all requested documents. This is a request for validation made pursuant to the Fair Debt Collection Practices Act. Please allow 30 days for processing after receive this information back.

Best Regards
Your Name
cc {Attorney Name}

Validation Letter – Insufficient/Partial Response

Date

Your Name
Address
City, State Zip

Debt Collector's Name
Address
City, State Zip

Re: Reference Number

Dear Debt Collector:

I received your so-called response to my request for validation and this does not prove anything. Validation is PROOF.

I do not see my signature on anything you provided, I didn't see anything proving that the balance you are attempting to collect is accurate, I didn't see anything showing your right to collect on this debt or your right to collect in my state!

I have documented my request and this joke of a response. If you continue to pursue collection activities on this invalidated account, including reporting nay account information to the credit bureaus, I will have no choice but to bring suit against your company and the original creditor for applicable damages under both the FDCPA and the FCRA.

This shall serve as your legal notice to cease and desist all communication with me in reference to this account, and that if any information is reporting on my credit report and/or causes me to be denied credit or more favorable terms, I will seek damages.

Regards

Your Name

Validation Letter – Medical

Date

Your Name
Address

Debt Collector's Name
Address

Dear Debt Collector:

I received a bill from you on (date), reference number (insert account number listed on letter) and I am disputing and requesting you to validate the debt. Per your letter, the debt is from (hospital/doctor), however, I am not aware of the amount due and your letter did not include a breakdown of fees.

I also do not remember giving permission to (name of doctor/hospital) to release my medical information to a third party. Under HIPAA law, my privacy and medical records should be protected from third parties. I was informed that HIPAA does allow for limited information to be released, therefore my request for validation should include the request for validation of the debt and HIPAA.

- Please provide a breakdown of fees, as well as any costs added for collection costs, late fees and medical charges.
- Please provide me with a copy of my signature with the provider of service to release my medical information to you.
- Please halt all reporting to the credit bureaus until the debt has been completely validated.

My current address is listed in this letter. I am in need of full documentation of everything you received from the provider who assigned you this debt. Please limit all communication with me to mail. This shall serve as your legal notice to cease and desist all communication with me in reference to this account.

Regards,
Full Name

Send to Credit Bureaus AFTER You've Sent A Validation Letter to Collection Agency & Haven't Received A Response/Sufficient Proof of the Debt

Date:

Your Name
Address

Credit Bureau Name
Address

Re: Name/Account # of Collection Agency as showing on your credit report

To Whom It May Concern:

I am in desperate need of your assistance. The above item is reporting on my credit report and I have no record of this debt or this company. I mailed them a letter (or letters) asking for more information on the account and was only sent an old bill showing a balance, but nothing more.

I have tried to have to account validated, but have not been successful. I've attached a copy of the letter sent to them and the certified mail receipt as proof of this. I am therefore, respectfully, asking for (insert credit bureau name) to delete this item from my credit report per FCRA and FDCPA guidelines.

Being that they were not able to prove the accuracy of this debt with me, I am not requesting for an investigation to be done, but rather the entire entry be deleted as there is no proof of its existence as proven by the attached documents.

Sincerely,
SIGN

(The credit bureaus will need a copy of ID docs showing proof of your address/SSN for identity protection purposes)

Validation Letter – When Another Collection Agency Buys An Invalidated Debt

Date

Your Name
Address
City, State Zip

Debt Collector's Name
Address
City, State Zip

Re: Reference Number

Dear Debt Collector:

I sent (Collection Agency #1) a dispute and demand for validation letter on (insert date); it was accepted by (insert name on signature confirmation card from post office) on (insert date from signature confirmation card from post office). Follow up letters were sent (if you did not send follow up letters leave blank).

Absent validation, both your company and (Collection Agency #1) are in violation of Federal Law for, but not limited to, continued collection activity on an invalidated debt pursuant to FDCPA § 809. Validation of debts [15 USC 1692g] (b).

My suggestion is that you return this account to (Collection Agency #1) and demand your money back, and/or compensation for time wasted pursuant to the "qualifying RECOURSE accounts provisions" of your purchase/assignment contract.

If any information about this alleged debt has been reported to the credit bureaus, I demand that you delete said information immediately, or I will have no choice but to take legal action against you for knowingly furnishing unverifiable information to the credit bureaus with the sole purpose of tarnishing my financial reputation. You have 5 days to remedy this matter.

Any further communication from you before I receive the demanded proof of this alleged debts' validity via federal and case law and I will instruct my attorney to begin drafting a formal complaint.

Regards,
Name

cc: Attorney's Name

Enclosures:
1) Copy of original and all subsequent validation demands
2) Copy of return receipts & signature confirmation cards

Appendix – Fair Debt Collection Practices Act

Appendix - FAIR DEBT COLLECTIONS PRACTICES ACT

Pay special attention to your rights in Sections 804-809

TITLE VIII - DEBT COLLECTION PRACTICES [Fair Debt Collection Practices Act]

§ 801. Short Title [15 USC 1601 note]

This title may be cited as the "Fair Debt Collection Practices Act."

§ 802. Congressional findings and declarations of purpose [15 USC 1692]

(a) There is abundant evidence of the use of abusive, deceptive, and unfair debt collection practices by many debt collectors. Abusive debt collection practices contribute to the number of personal bankruptcies, to marital instability, to the loss of jobs, and to invasions of individual privacy.

(b) Existing laws and procedures for redressing these injuries are inadequate to protect consumers.

(c) Means other than misrepresentation or other abusive debt collection practices are available for the effective collection of debts.

(d) Abusive debt collection practices are carried on to a substantial extent in interstate commerce and through means and instrumentalities of such commerce. Even where abusive debt collection practices are purely intrastate in character, they nevertheless directly affect interstate commerce.

(e) It is the purpose of this title to eliminate abusive debt collection practices by debt collectors, to insure that those debt collectors who refrain from using abusive debt collection practices are not competitively disadvantaged, and to promote consistent State action to protect consumers against debt collection abuses.

§ 803. Definitions [15 USC 1692a]

As used in this title --

(1) The term "Commission" means the Federal Trade Commission.

(2) The term "communication" means the conveying of information regarding a debt directly or indirectly to any person through any medium.

(3) The term "consumer" means any natural person obligated or allegedly obligated to pay any debt.

(4) The term "creditor" means any person who offers or extends credit creating a debt or to whom a debt is owed, but such term does not include any person to the extent that he receives an assignment or transfer of a debt in default solely for the purpose of facilitating collection of such debt for another.

(5) The term "debt" means any obligation or alleged obligation of a consumer to pay money arising out of a transaction in which the money, property, insurance or services which are the subject of the transaction are primarily for personal, family, or household purposes, whether or not such obligation has been reduced to judgment.

(6) The term "debt collector" means any person who uses any instrumentality of interstate commerce or the mails in any business the principal purpose of which is

the collection of any debts, or who regularly collects or attempts to collect, directly or indirectly, debts owed or due or asserted to be owed or due another. Notwithstanding the exclusion provided by clause (F) of the last sentence of this paragraph, the term includes any creditor who, in the process of collecting his own debts, uses any name other than his own which would indicate that a third person is collecting or attempting to collect such debts. For the purpose of section 808(6), such term also includes any person who uses any instrumentality of interstate commerce or the mails in any business the principal purpose of which is the enforcement of security interests. The term does not include --

(A) any officer or employee of a creditor while, in the name of the creditor, collecting debts for such creditor;

(B) any person while acting as a debt collector for another person, both of whom are related by common ownership or affiliated by corporate control, if the person acting as a debt collector does so only for persons to whom it is so related or affiliated and if the principal business of such person is not the collection of debts;

(C) any officer or employee of the United States or any State to the extent that collecting or attempting to collect any debt is in the performance of his official duties;

(D) any person while serving or attempting to serve legal process on any other person in connection with the judicial enforcement of any debt;

(E) any nonprofit organization which, at the request of consumers, performs bona fide consumer credit counseling and assists consumers in the liquidation of their debts by receiving payments from such consumers and distributing such amounts to creditors; and

(F) any person collecting or attempting to collect any debt owed or due or asserted to be owed or due another to the extent such activity (i) is incidental to a bona fide fiduciary obligation or a bona fide escrow arrangement; (ii) concerns a debt which was originated by such person; (iii) concerns a debt which was not in default at the time it was obtained by such person; or (iv) concerns a debt obtained by such person as a secured party in a commercial credit transaction involving the creditor.

(7) The term "location information" means a consumer's place of abode and his telephone number at such place, or his place of employment.

(8) The term "State" means any State, territory, or possession of the United States, the District of Columbia, the Commonwealth of Puerto Rico, or any political subdivision of any of the foregoing.

§ 804. Acquisition of location information [15 USC 1692b]

Any debt collector communicating with any person other than the consumer for the purpose of acquiring location information about the consumer shall --

(1) identify himself, state that he is confirming or correcting location information concerning the consumer, and, only if expressly requested, identify his employer;

(2) not state that such consumer owes any debt;

(3) not communicate with any such person more than once unless requested to do so by such person or

unless the debt collector reasonably believes that the earlier response of such person is erroneous or incomplete and that such person now has correct or complete location information;

(4) not communicate by post card;

(5) not use any language or symbol on any envelope or in the contents of any communication effected by the mails or telegram that indicates that the debt collector is in the debt collection business or that the communication relates to the collection of a debt; and

(6) after the debt collector knows the consumer is represented by an attorney with regard to the subject debt and has knowledge of, or can readily ascertain, such attorney's name and address, not communicate with any person other than that attorney, unless the attorney fails to respond within a reasonable period of time to the communication from the debt collector.

§ 805. Communication in connection with debt collection   [15 USC 1692c]

(a) COMMUNICATION WITH THE CONSUMER GENERALLY. Without the prior consent of the consumer given directly to the debt collector or the express permission of a court of competent jurisdiction, a debt collector may not communicate with a consumer in connection with the collection of any debt --

(1) at any unusual time or place or a time or place known or which should be known to be inconvenient to the consumer. In the absence of knowledge of circumstances to the contrary, a debt collector shall assume that the convenient time for communicating with a consumer is after 8 o'clock antimeridian and before 9 o'clock postmeridian, local time at the consumer's location;

(2) if the debt collector knows the consumer is represented by an attorney with respect to such debt and has knowledge of, or can readily ascertain, such attorney's name and address, unless the attorney fails to respond within a reasonable period of time to a communication from the debt collector or unless the attorney consents to direct communication with the consumer; or

(3) at the consumer's place of employment if the debt collector knows or has reason to know that the consumer's employer prohibits the consumer from receiving such communication.

(b) COMMUNICATION WITH THIRD PARTIES. Except as provided in section 804, without the prior consent of the consumer given directly to the debt collector, or the express permission of a court of competent jurisdiction, or as reasonably necessary to effectuate a postjudgment judicial remedy, a debt collector may not communicate, in connection with the collection of any debt, with any person other than a consumer, his attorney, a consumer reporting agency if otherwise permitted by law, the creditor, the attorney of the creditor, or the attorney of the debt collector.

(c) CEASING COMMUNICATION. If a consumer notifies a debt collector in writing that the consumer refuses to pay a debt or that the consumer wishes the debt collector to cease further communication with the consumer, the debt collector shall not communicate further with the consumer with respect to such debt, except --

(1) to advise the consumer that the debt collector's further efforts are being terminated;

(2) to notify the consumer that the debt collector or creditor may invoke specified remedies which are ordinarily invoked by such debt collector or creditor; or

(3) where applicable, to notify the consumer that the debt collector or creditor intends to invoke a specified remedy.

If such notice from the consumer is made by mail, notification shall be complete upon receipt.

(d) For the purpose of this section, the term "consumer" includes the consumer's spouse, parent (if the consumer is a minor), guardian, executor, or administrator.

§ 806. Harassment or abuse [15 USC 1692d]

A debt collector may not engage in any conduct the natural consequence of which is to harass, oppress, or abuse any person in connection with the collection of a debt. Without limiting the general application of the foregoing, the following conduct is a violation of this section:

(1) The use or threat of use of violence or other criminal means to harm the physical person, reputation, or property of any person.

(2) The use of obscene or profane language or language the natural consequence of which is to abuse the hearer or reader.

(3) The publication of a list of consumers who allegedly refuse to pay debts, except to a consumer reporting agency or to persons meeting the requirements of section 603(f) or 604(3)1 of this Act.

(4) The advertisement for sale of any debt to coerce payment of the debt.

(5) Causing a telephone to ring or engaging any person in telephone conversation repeatedly or continuously with intent to annoy, abuse, or harass any person at the called number.

(6) Except as provided in section 804, the placement of telephone calls without meaningful disclosure of the caller's identity.

§ 807. False or misleading representations [15 USC 1692e]

A debt collector may not use any false, deceptive, or misleading representation or means in connection with the collection of any debt. Without limiting the general application of the foregoing, the following conduct is a violation of this section:

(1) The false representation or implication that the debt collector is vouched for, bonded by, or affiliated with the United States or any State, including the use of any badge, uniform, or facsimile thereof.

(2) The false representation of --

(A) the character, amount, or legal status of any debt; or

(B) any services rendered or compensation which may be lawfully received by any debt collector for the collection of a debt.

(3) The false representation or implication that any individual is an attorney or that any communication is from an attorney.

(4) The representation or implication that nonpayment of any debt will result in the arrest or imprisonment of

any person or the seizure, garnishment, attachment, or sale of any property or wages of any person unless such action is lawful and the debt collector or creditor intends to take such action.

(5) The threat to take any action that cannot legally be taken or that is not intended to be taken.

(6) The false representation or implication that a sale, referral, or other transfer of any interest in a debt shall cause the consumer to --

(A) lose any claim or defense to payment of the debt; or

(B) become subject to any practice prohibited by this title.

(7) The false representation or implication that the consumer committed any crime or other conduct in order to disgrace the consumer.

(8) Communicating or threatening to communicate to any person credit information which is known or which should be known to be false, including the failure to communicate that a disputed debt is disputed.

(9) The use or distribution of any written communication which simulates or is falsely represented to be a document authorized, issued, or approved by any court, official, or agency of the United States or any State, or which creates a false impression as to its source, authorization, or approval.

(10) The use of any false representation or deceptive means to collect or attempt to collect any debt or to obtain information concerning a consumer.

(11) The failure to disclose in the initial written communication with the consumer and, in addition, if

the initial communication with the consumer is oral, in that initial oral communication, that the debt collector is attempting to collect a debt and that any information obtained will be used for that purpose, and the failure to disclose in subsequent communications that the communication is from a debt collector, except that this paragraph shall not apply to a formal pleading made in connection with a legal action.

(12) The false representation or implication that accounts have been turned over to innocent purchasers for value.

(13) The false representation or implication that documents are legal process.

(14) The use of any business, company, or organization name other than the true name of the debt collector's business, company, or organization.

(15) The false representation or implication that documents are not legal process forms or do not require action by the consumer.

(16) The false representation or implication that a debt collector operates or is employed by a consumer reporting agency as defined by section 603(f) of this Act.

§ 808. Unfair practices [15 USC 1692f]

A debt collector may not use unfair or unconscionable means to collect or attempt to collect any debt. Without limiting the general application of the foregoing, the following conduct is a violation of this section:

(1) The collection of any amount (including any interest, fee, charge, or expense incidental to the principal obligation) unless such amount is expressly authorized by the agreement creating the debt or permitted by law.

(2) The acceptance by a debt collector from any person of a check or other payment instrument postdated by more than five days unless such person is notified in writing of the debt collector's intent to deposit such check or instrument not more than ten nor less than three business days prior to such deposit.

(3) The solicitation by a debt collector of any postdated check or other postdated payment instrument for the purpose of threatening or instituting criminal prosecution.

(4) Depositing or threatening to deposit any postdated check or other postdated payment instrument prior to the date on such check or instrument.

(5) Causing charges to be made to any person for communications by concealment of the true purpose of the communication. Such charges include, but are not limited to, collect telephone calls and telegram fees.

(6) Taking or threatening to take any nonjudicial action to effect dispossession or disablement of property if --

(A) there is no present right to possession of the property claimed as collateral through an enforceable security interest;

(B) there is no present intention to take possession of the property; or

(C) the property is exempt by law from such dispossession or disablement.

(7) Communicating with a consumer regarding a debt by post card.

(8) Using any language or symbol, other than the debt collector's address, on any envelope when

communicating with a consumer by use of the mails or by telegram, except that a debt collector may use his business name if such name does not indicate that he is in the debt collection business.

§ 809. Validation of debts   [15 USC 1692g]

(a) Within five days after the initial communication with a consumer in connection with the collection of any debt, a debt collector shall, unless the following information is contained in the initial communication or the consumer has paid the debt, send the consumer a written notice containing --

(1) the amount of the debt;

(2) the name of the creditor to whom the debt is owed;

(3) a statement that unless the consumer, within thirty days after receipt of the notice, disputes the validity of the debt, or any portion thereof, the debt will be assumed to be valid by the debt collector;

(4) a statement that if the consumer notifies the debt collector in writing within the thirty-day period that the debt, or any portion thereof, is disputed, the debt collector will obtain verification of the debt or a copy of a judgment against the consumer and a copy of such verification or judgment will be mailed to the consumer by the debt collector; and

(5) a statement that, upon the consumer's written request within the thirty-day period, the debt collector will provide the consumer with the name and address of the original creditor, if different from the current creditor.

(b) If the consumer notifies the debt collector in writing within the thirty-day period described in subsection (a) that the debt, or any portion thereof, is disputed, or that the consumer requests the name and address of the original creditor, the debt collector shall cease collection of the debt, or any disputed portion thereof, until the debt collector obtains verification of the debt or any copy of a judgment, or the name and address of the original creditor, and a copy of such verification or judgment, or name and address of the original creditor, is mailed to the consumer by the debt collector.

(c) The failure of a consumer to dispute the validity of a debt under this section may not be construed by any court as an admission of liability by the consumer.

§ 810. Multiple debts [15 USC 1692h]

If any consumer owes multiple debts and makes any single payment to any debt collector with respect to such debts, such debt collector may not apply such payment to any debt which is disputed by the consumer and, where applicable, shall apply such payment in accordance with the consumer's directions.

§ 811. Legal actions by debt collectors [15 USC 1692i]

(a) Any debt collector who brings any legal action on a debt against any consumer shall --

(1) in the case of an action to enforce an interest in real property securing the consumer's obligation, bring such action only in a judicial district or similar legal entity in which such real property is located; or

(2) in the case of an action not described in paragraph (1), bring such action only in the judicial district or similar legal entity --

(A) in which such consumer signed the contract sued upon; or

(B) in which such consumer resides at the commencement of the action.

(b) Nothing in this title shall be construed to authorize the bringing of legal actions by debt collectors.

§ 812. Furnishing certain deceptive forms [15 USC 1692j]

(a) It is unlawful to design, compile, and furnish any form knowing that such form would be used to create the false belief in a consumer that a person other than the creditor of such consumer is participating in the collection of or in an attempt to collect a debt such consumer allegedly owes such creditor, when in fact such person is not so participating.

(b) Any person who violates this section shall be liable to the same extent and in the same manner as a debt collector is liable under section 813 for failure to comply with a provision of this title.

§ 813. Civil liability [15 USC 1692k]

(a) Except as otherwise provided by this section, any debt collector who fails to comply with any provision of this title with respect to any person is liable to such person in an amount equal to the sum of --

(1) any actual damage sustained by such person as a result of such failure;

(2) (A) in the case of any action by an individual, such additional damages as the court may allow, but not exceeding $1,000; or

(B) in the case of a class action, (i) such amount for each named plaintiff as could be recovered under subparagraph (A), and (ii) such amount as the court may allow for all other class members, without regard to a minimum individual recovery, not to exceed the lesser of $500,000 or 1 per centum of the net worth of the debt collector; and

(3) in the case of any successful action to enforce the foregoing liability, the costs of the action, together with a reasonable attorney's fee as determined by the court. On a finding by the court that an action under this section was brought in bad faith and for the purpose of harassment, the court may award to the defendant attorney's fees reasonable in relation to the work expended and costs.

(b) In determining the amount of liability in any action under subsection (a), the court shall consider, among other relevant factors --

(1) in any individual action under subsection (a)(2)(A), the frequency and persistence of noncompliance by the debt collector, the nature of such noncompliance, and the extent to which such noncompliance was intentional; or

(2) in any class action under subsection (a)(2)(B), the frequency and persistence of noncompliance by the debt collector, the nature of such noncompliance, the resources of the debt collector, the number of persons adversely affected, and the extent to which the debt collector's noncompliance was intentional.

(c) A debt collector may not be held liable in any action brought under this title if the debt collector shows by a preponderance of evidence that the violation was not intentional and resulted from a bona fide error notwithstanding the maintenance of procedures reasonably adapted to avoid any such error.

(d) An action to enforce any liability created by this title may be brought in any appropriate United States district court without regard to the amount in controversy, or in any other court of competent jurisdiction, within one year from the date on which the violation occurs.

(e) No provision of this section imposing any liability shall apply to any act done or omitted in good faith in conformity with any advisory opinion of the Commission, notwithstanding that after such act or omission has occurred, such opinion is amended, rescinded, or determined by judicial or other authority to be invalid for any reason.

§ 814. Administrative enforcement   [15 USC 1692l]

(a) Compliance with this title shall be enforced by the Commission, except to the extend that enforcement of the requirements imposed under this title is specifically committed to another agency under subsection (b). For purpose of the exercise by the Commission of its functions and powers under the Federal Trade Commission Act, a violation of this title shall be deemed an unfair or deceptive act or practice in violation of that Act. All of the functions and powers of the Commission under the Federal Trade Commission Act are available to the Commission to enforce compliance by any person with this title, irrespective of whether that person is engaged in commerce or meets any other jurisdictional tests in the Federal Trade Commission Act, including the power to enforce the provisions of this title in the same manner as if the violation had been a violation of a Federal Trade Commission trade regulation rule.

(b) Compliance with any requirements imposed under this title shall be enforced under --

(1) section 8 of the Federal Deposit Insurance Act, in the case of --

(A) national banks, by the Comptroller of the Currency;

(B) member banks of the Federal Reserve System (other than national banks), by the Federal Reserve Board; and

(C) banks the deposits or accounts of which are insured by the Federal Deposit Insurance Corporation (other than members of the Federal Reserve System), by the Board of Directors of the Federal Deposit Insurance Corporation;

(2) section 5(d) of the Home Owners Loan Act of 1933, section 407 of the National Housing Act, and sections 6(i) and 17 of the Federal Home Loan Bank Act, by the Federal Home Loan Bank Board (acting directing or through the Federal Savings and Loan Insurance Corporation), in the case of any institution subject to any of those provisions;

(3) the Federal Credit Union Act, by the Administrator of the National Credit Union Administration with respect to any Federal credit union;

(4) subtitle IV of Title 49, by the Interstate Commerce Commission with respect to any common carrier subject to such subtitle;

(5) the Federal Aviation Act of 1958, by the Secretary of Transportation with respect to any air carrier or any foreign air carrier subject to that Act; and

(6) the Packers and Stockyards Act, 1921 (except as provided in section 406 of that Act), by the Secretary of Agriculture with respect to any activities subject to that Act.

(c) For the purpose of the exercise by any agency referred to in subsection (b) of its powers under any Act referred to in that subsection, a violation of any requirement imposed under this title shall be deemed to be a violation of a requirement imposed under that Act. In addition to its powers under any provision of law specifically referred to in subsection (b), each of the agencies referred to in that subsection may exercise, for the purpose of enforcing compliance with any requirement imposed under this title any other authority conferred on it by law, except as provided in subsection (d).

(d) Neither the Commission nor any other agency referred to in subsection (b) may promulgate trade regulation rules or other regulations with respect to the collection of debts by debt collectors as defined in this title.

§ 815. Reports to Congress by the Commission [15 USC 1692m]

(a) Not later than one year after the effective date of this title and at one-year intervals thereafter, the Commission shall make reports to the Congress concerning the administration of its functions under this title, including such recommendations as the Commission deems necessary or appropriate. In addition, each report of the Commission shall include its assessment of the extent to which compliance with this title is being achieved and a summary of the enforcement actions taken by the Commission under section 814 of this title.

(b) In the exercise of its functions under this title, the Commission may obtain upon request the views of any other Federal agency which exercises enforcement functions under section 814 of this title.

§ 816. Relation to State laws [15 USC 1692n]

This title does not annul, alter, or affect, or exempt any person subject to the provisions of this title from complying with the laws of any State with respect to debt collection practices, except to the extent that those laws are inconsistent with any provision of this title, and then only to the extent of the inconsistency. For purposes of this section, a State law is not inconsistent with this title if the protection such law affords any consumer is greater than the protection provided by this title.

§ 817. Exemption for State regulation [15 USC 1692o]

The Commission shall by regulation exempt from the requirements of this title any class of debt collection practices within any State if the Commission determines that under the law of that State that class of debt collection practices is subject to requirements substantially similar to those imposed by this title, and that there is adequate provision for enforcement.

§ 818. Effective date [15 USC 1692 note]

This title takes effect upon the expiration of six months after the date of its enactment, but section 809 shall apply only with respect to debts for which the initial attempt to collect occurs after such effective date.

Appendix – SOL

Appendix – Statute of Limitations (Section of State's Legislature Included)

STATE	WRITTEN	ORAL	PROMISSORY	OPEN	STATE CODE
Alabama	3	6	6	3	§6.2.37
Alaska	3	6	3	3	§4-3-118
Arizona	6	3	5	3	§09.10.053
Arkansas	5	3	3	5	HB 2412
California	4	2	4	4	§337
Colorado	6	6	6	6	§13-80-103.5
Connecticut	6	3	6	6	Ch. 926 Sec. 52-576
Delaware	3	3	3	3	Title 10 Sec.8106
D.C.	3	3	3	3	§12-301
Florida	5	4	5	4	§95.11

Georgia	6	4	6	4 or 6**	§9-3-25
Hawaii	6	6	6	6	HRS 657-1(4)
Idaho	5	4	5	5	§614.1.5
Illinois	10	5	10	5 or 10***	§5-216
Indiana	10	6	10	6	735 ILCS 5/13-206
Iowa	10	5	5	10	§34-11-2-9
Kansas	3	3	3	3	§60-512
Kentucky	15	5	15	5 or 15****	§413.120 & 413.090
Louisiana	3	10	10	3	§2-3494-4
Maine	6	6	6	6	§14-205-752
Maryland`	3	3	6	3	§5-101
Massachusetts	6	6	6	6	§260-2
Michigan	6	6	6	6	§600.5807.8
Minnesota	6	6	6	6	§541.05
Mississippi	3	3	3	3	§516.120

State				
Missouri	5	5	5	5	§15-1-29
Montana	8	5	8	8	22-2-207
Nebraska	4	4	4	4	§1-52.1
Nevada	4	4	4	4	28-01-16
New Hampshire	3	3	3	3	§25-206
New Jersey	6	6	6	6	382-A:3-118
New Mexico	4	4	4	4	2A:14-1
New York	6	6	6	6	§37-1-4
North Carolina	3	3	5	3	NRS 11.190
North Dakota	6	6	6	6	§2-213
Ohio	6	6	6	6	§2305.07
Oklahoma	5	3	5	3 or 5****	§12-95A(1), (2)
Oregon	6	6	6	6	§12.08
Pennsylvania	4	4	4	4	42 Pa. C.S.5525(a)
Rhode Island	10	10	10	10	§6A-2-725

South Carolina	10	10	3	3	SEC 15-3-530
South Dakota	6	3	6	6	15-2-13
Tennessee	6	6	6	6	28-3-109
Texas	4	4	4	4	§16.004
Utah	6	4	6	4	78-12-25
Vermont	5	3	6	3	8.01-246
Virginia	6	6	5	6	§9A-3-118
Washington	6	3	6	6	4.16.040
West Virginia	10	10	10	10	893.43
Wisconsin	6	6	10	6	§55-2-6
Wyoming	10	8	10	8	§1-3-105

Written contracts are when you agree to pay back a loan under the terms written in the document you and the creditor have signed.

Promissory Notes are written contracts with scheduled payments and interest on the loan, such as student loans and mortgages

Oral Contracts are when you agree to repay the money loaned to you by someone, it's a verbal agreement

Open-Ended contracts are revolving lines of credit who's balances will vary, depending on usage, from month to month, such as credit cards.

Resources

Resources

All of the information provided in this text can be found on the websites listed below. As I mentioned from the onset, financial literacy is POWER. Ensuring that you are being educated from the right place is also important, which is why I stick to state and federal government websites for the most up-to-date and accurate information.

Urban Institue Study:
www.urban.org/research/publication/delinquent-debt-america/view/full_report

Consumer Financial Protection Bureau: www.cfpb.org

Fair Trade Commission: www.ftc.org
www.ftc.gov/news-events/audio-video/video/life-debt-data-integrity-debt-collection-part-4

Consumer Finance:
files.consumerfinance.gov/f/201210_cfpb_debt-collection-final-rule.pdf

Protecting Consumer Rights:
www.protectingconsumerrights.com

Bankrate.com (SOL Chart):
http://www.bankrate.com/finance/credit-cards/state-statutes-of-limitations-for-old-debts-1.aspx

Privacy Rights: www.privacyrights.org

Your State's Attorney General's Office